Unless I See . . .

2nd Edition

Unless I See . . .

Reasons to Consider the Christian Faith

2nd Edition

PATRICK Y. ZUKERAN

Dedication

This book is dedicated to my wife Kris,
for all her love, understanding, and support.

Contents

Foreword

What would it take for you to believe the message of the Bible? When I ask that question of skeptics on campus or in society, often they respond by saying "I won't believe in the gospel, unless I see . . ." This book is for them, as well as for those with honest questions and doubts.

Pat Zukeran takes on the key questions and key issues. He delves into questions of our existence and God's existence. He tackles questions about the Bible. Is it historically accurate? Is it inspired? Is there proof outside the Bible for its authenticity? And he focuses time and attention on the person of Jesus Christ. What about His claims to deity? How did He validate those claims to deity? Aren't there other ways to heaven? Is Jesus the only way?

Any atheist, agnostic, skeptic, or honest seeker will find this clear and concise book a challenge to their own unbelief or doubt. Pat Zukeran takes on the philosophical challenges against Christianity and marshals compelling evidence for the Christian faith.

I invite you to read this book with an open mind. If you think the evidence AGAINST Christianity is overwhelming, then read on and discover that it is the evidence FOR Christianity that is overwhelming.

Kerby Anderson
President, Probe Ministries International

Preface

The Bible gives us a glimpse into the lives of real people with whom we can identify. Jesus had twelve devoted followers called the twelve Apostles. Upon reading the gospels, a reader will often realize he or she can relate to a particular one of the Apostles. Some identify with Peter, courageous and noble, yet sometimes brash and hot tempered. Others connect with John and James, the sons of thunder. This pair once desired to destroy a town for rejecting their message. There are still others who relate to Paul, the scholar and evangelist to those outside the Jewish race and Israel. He was educated in the finest schools of Israel and regularly debated the great scholars of his time.

I identify most with Thomas, the skeptic who demanded concrete proof before committing to a new belief. After many proclaimed that Jesus had risen from the dead he resisted, saying, "Unless I see the nail marks in his hands and put my finger where the nails were, and put my finger into his side, I will not believe."

I felt the same way. Even after receiving Christ as my Lord and savior, some nagging questions began to undermine my new faith. Although I wanted Christianity to be true, there were too many facts that seemed to discredit its claims. Like Thomas, I thought, "Unless I see, I will not believe."

Then God made Himself real to me. In His own way He proved to me the reality and credibility of the Bible's and Jesus' claims: the nail prints and pierced side that I needed to touch.

Acknowledgements

This book is the product of many who love God and passionately desire for others to come to a saving knowledge of His Son, Jesus Christ. Their labor of love and dedication to the Lord made this work possible. I would like to express my appreciation to Dr. Danny Yamashiro, Reef Makue, and the staff of Jesus Christ is Calling You ministry inspiring me to write this book and supporting me in the entire process. I thank the Lord for the partnership we have in ministry as evangelists of our Lord.

I would like to express my gratitude to my personal advisory team: Fouad Bashour, B. J. Cope, Nelson Lin, Daniel Ma, Kevin Pon, and William Yiu for their friendship and daily assistance. I would also like to thank Deanne Closson, Jeff Liaw, Theresa Nichols, and Marina Wong for their perseverance in the editing process.

"I thank my God every time I remember you. In all my prayers for all of you, I always pray with joy because of your partnership in the gospel from the first day until now, ..."

(Philippians 1:3–5)

Introduction

A solitary figure sat alone in the restaurant gazing at the sea. As the morning sun glared off the water he watched the fishermen scurry to and from their boats, some carrying fish and others following with nets slung over their shoulders. There was a lot to think about. One associate had committed suicide, and the leader, to whom he had entrusted his life and future, lay rotting in a nearby grave. Was it all a mirage? Was it just an emotional experience that drew the heart of this young man away from his family and future dreams to follow a new hope? What had he done, and how would he put his life back together now?

He took one last sip, paid for his meal and departed the restaurant. As he stepped out of the restaurant, the sun rested directly above his head. It was noon. As he adjusted his eyes to the sunlight, he heard three men calling his name.

"Thomas! Thomas!" they shouted running toward him. With excitement in their voices and joy beaming out of their eyes, they bounded to him.

No, not them! he thought. He did not want to have anything to do with these ten men again.

"We have seen the risen Lord!" they cried with childish exuberance. Peter grabbed a firm hold of Thomas' left sleeve and placed his other hand on his shoulder and looked right into Thomas' eyes. "Thomas, it's true! He's alive! Jesus has risen from the dead just like He said He would. Indeed, He is God incarnate! He is the Messiah we have been waiting for! He spoke with us and I even touched him with these hands!" Peter exclaimed holding up his hands for Thomas to see. Peter's stare and tone of voice were very convincing, yet that was Peter. He was always the persuasive one.

Thomas gazed into the exuberant eyes of Peter and then turned away. "No," he said taking a few steps away from the men. "As much as I would love to believe this, I cannot. You men go on. I've got things to do."

I cannot get caught up in the emotion, Thomas thought to himself. *I will not devote my entire life and sacrifice my family and future again for something I cannot see.* Thomas slowly trudged down the street.

His closest associate, John, shouted, "Thomas, wait!" Thomas turned around and saw his friend scurrying toward him. "Thomas, what will it take for you to believe?" John asked.

Thomas looked into the sincere and caring eyes of his best friend. He momentarily took a deep breath and stated, "Unless I see the nail marks in his hands and put my hand into his side, I will not believe it."

John understood his friend. Thomas was always the honest one. Of course it would be difficult for Thomas to believe in a dead man rising to life. John understood Thomas' response. "Thomas, come with us. Hear the others. They have seen him too," John pleaded.

"All the talking and stories won't convince me, John. I need proof! I am not going to just take your word for it, show me the evidence!" Thomas replied angrily.

John put his right hand on Thomas' shoulder and with the love of a concerned brother he gently urged his friend, "Come with us one last time. I know how you feel, Thomas. I felt the same way when the women told me. I ran to his grave and when it was empty, I did not know what to make of it. But Thomas, we have all seen the risen Lord! Jesus is alive! He is the savior of the world! Come, just this final time and listen to what we have to say."

It was not his words that coaxed Thomas into agreeing. It

was the love and kindred spirit of his friend John that made him reluctantly consent. "Alright," he said, "But this is the final time I will meet with you." Grudgingly, Thomas joined the other three and began walking with them to the house. *Could it be true?* Thomas thought to himself. *Could Jesus really be alive?* He paused and then made this resolve in his heart. *Unless I see, I will not believe!*

My Search

I was a junior in high school when I first heard it said that God was interested in my life. He wanted to have a relationship with me that would bring me joy, peace, and rest from the trials of the world. "Could it be true?" I asked myself.

I had been up till the early hours of the morning the night before, hanging out with friends. Now at the 10 a.m. service I struggled to keep my eyes open. Finally losing the struggle after the third hymn, I napped peacefully in the pew. I would have loved to have stayed in that comatose position, but something woke me. As I rubbed my eyes and gathered my senses, I realized the pastor was standing behind a table upon which rested bread and grape juice. This would be my first encounter with the Christian ceremony of Communion.

The pastor explained this tradition to us. It was to commemorate the final supper Jesus had with His disciples, before His sacrificial death on the cross that was to pay the price for the sins of the world. Then the pastor quoted two verses. I can still hear the voice of that elderly man declare, "Jesus said, 'Come unto me all who are weary and heavy laden and I will give you rest.'" I woke up and sat up in my chair intrigued by what I had just heard. *God wanted to be a part of my life? He wanted a personal relationship with me? He cared so much about me that He wanted to carry the burdens of my life and give me rest?* As a junior in high school, I was dealing with adolescent insecurities, relational difficulties, poor grades, and an uncertain future. No one was interested in my turmoil filled situation. Everyone had pain of their own to deal with, so the preacher's words were new to me. I believed in a God of some kind, but I had never considered that He would care for me.

Then the pastor read the second verse, "Jesus said, '. . . and I will be with you always, even unto the end of the age.'" My interest continued to grow. Not only does the God of the universe care about me, but He promises never to abandon me even in my worst moments. Life can be lonely in times of great difficulty. Was it really true that God wanted to be with me?

The pastor gave the invitation, "If you would like to have a relationship with God and receive Christ as your Lord and Savior and have the assurance of eternal life with Him, repeat this prayer." The pastor led us in the prayer to receive Christ. I remember sitting in my pew and praying, "God, if this is real, if these promises are true and you are the kind of God described in the Bible, I receive you as my Lord and Savior." It is then I accepted Christ and became a child of God.

I did not grow up in church, but I attended an Episcopalian school so I had heard some of the Bible, but never had I heard or understood it in this way. So I reported this exciting news to my school priest that Monday. With very little emotion, he acknowledged my story and then told me not to take the Bible so seriously. He pointed out there are many details and stories that are not accurate nor should they be taken seriously. I began to seriously question my newborn faith. In my high school Bible class, I learned rational explanations for the miracles of the Bible and the errors in history, chronology, authorship, and archaeology that cast its authenticity in doubt.

Several history and liberal Christian textbooks presented

some of these findings, which appeared to be very convincing. For example, Moses' crossing of the Red Sea occurred at the Sea of Reeds. Some areas of this sea are only three feet deep. Any group of people could have easily made this crossing. Daniel was not written in 500 B.C. as the book claims but written much later in the second century B.C. because it contains Greek and Aramaic, languages unknown to a Jewish writer of Daniel's time. Therefore the book is not really prophetic, it simply was given that appearance to encourage the Jewish people, who were suffering under Roman persecution. History books stated that the resurrection was a legend. The disciples wanted the words of Jesus to be true. The hope of the heavenly kingdom and the words of eternal life had to continue in order for the movement to grow. As His followers gathered, they felt His warm presence in a real way and went forth to preach a "risen Jesus" to a world in need of hope, even if their story was convoluted and contrived. Since many were in foreign lands, there was no way the converts could confirm or deny the message. Many took it by faith. It did not matter that Jesus' body was in the grave, the disciples were sincere and their message of hope changed the world.

These conclusions cast serious doubt on the credibility of the Christian faith. It seemed that Christianity was another nice story, but no one should not be foolish enough to buy into all it's claims. I searched for answers but no one seemed to have them. My faith began to wane. I so wished to believe in the God of the Bible but my new faith seemed to be just another emotional experience. I refused to dedicate my life to a religion that said, "You just have to take a leap of faith." I needed to see the nail prints in Jesus' hands and feel His side. I said to myself, "Unless I see, I will not believe."

After months of questioning, I sat at a restaurant with one of my friends from church. He looked at my discouraged countenance and said, "I do not have the answers but this book may be able to help you." He gave me a copy of *Evidence That Demands a Verdict* by Josh McDowell. I read it thoroughly. Then I read another book and then another. My quest for the truth had begun.

This is the story of my search. For those who are saying, "Unless I see, I cannot believe," I hope this journey will reveal the "nail prints in the hands" and the "pierced side" of Jesus, God's Son.

Chapter 1
See a Hopeless Future

*T*here are three questions every human being must consider. Of all the creatures on earth, man alone must inevitably wrestle with "Who am I?", "Why am I here?", and "Where am I going?" Your answers determine your moral standards, your life goals, and your approach to the future, including its inevitable end. Your world view will determine how you answer these questions.

Man once answered these questions based on his understanding of a Creator. That all changed with the Enlightenment. A new world view engulfed western culture where science and human reason became the chief measure of truth. Many influential thinkers discarded religion like an old garment and replaced it with the finer garments of Enlightenment thinking. As a result, man sought answers without reference to God. However, as he studied and refined his conclusions, he discovered them to be dark and terrifying.

Who Am I?

How does an atheist answer the question, "Who am I?" Atheists will often attribute great value to humanity, but they don't have a logical reason for that intrinsic meaning. Most atheist believe the universe is the result of an accident. It is a product of an accidental atomic explosion, the "Big Bang." The ultimate source of the universe is the result of a mindless collision of atoms.

Cosmologist Victor Stenger states, ". . . physicists are now claiming that the hundreds of billions of stars and galaxies, including the earth and humanity, are not conscious creations but an accident. There is no creator, because there was no creation."[1] The universe exists with no real purpose because it is the result of a chance-driven process. Its existence is a fluke, not a planned outcome with no intelligent design behind it.

From a random combination of atoms colliding and combining a solar system, a sun and planet earth were formed. After millions of years and the "luck of the draw", electricity and gases produced water. From this primordial soup, life accidentally arose. This theory is stated in the National Association of Biology Teachers 1995 Official Position Statement:

> The diversity of life is the outcome of evolution: an unsupervised, impersonal, unpredictable and natural process of temporal descent with genetic modification that is affected by natural selection, chance, historical contingencies and changing environments.[2]

Accepting this origin explanation, we must conclude that since the universe was an accident, then man must be one as well. Indeed, many would admit it. Even evolutionist George Gaylord Simpson states, "Man is the result of a purposeless and natural process that did not have him in mind."[3]

Let us bring this down to a personal level in order to answer the question "Who am I?". You and I are here merely by chance. We are the result of a mindless and purposeless process. We are really an insignificant object in a vast universe. We arrived accidentally for no ultimate reason, we exist for a fleeting

[1] Victor Stenger, "Was the Universe Created?" *Free Inquiry*, Summer 1987, p.26.

[2] *The American Biology Teacher*, vol. 58, January 1996, p. 61-62.

[3] George Simpson, *The Meaning of Evolution* (New Haven, Conn.: Yale University Press, 1967), p. 344-345.

moment in the expanse of time, and soon become extinct and forgotten forever in the dark expanse of space. This premise leads to some important ideas about the meaning of life for each individual.

Why Am I Here?

For the atheists who reject the existence of God, the final reality is that the universe has no purpose, mankind has no ultimate purpose. Therefore if the universe has no purpose, then man cannot have intrinsic purpose; the bottom line is an empty life.

The universe exists with no ultimate purpose because it is the result of random chance; it was an accident. Another way of looking at the issue is to suppose the Big Bang never occurred. What ultimate difference would it have made if the universe existed or not? Scientists now know that the universe is still expanding and will one day cease. When that happens, what difference will it make that our universe was even here?

So if the universe is an accident, then what about mankind? Man becomes merely the result of a mindless evolutionary process. We are an accident composed of matter produced by chance. There is no more meaning to our existence than that of a fly. As the universe will one day cease to exist, mankind will cease to exist. What difference will there be for his existence in a dying universe?

Some will reject this tenet arguing, "My life makes a difference to my family or the legacy I leave for those who come after me." This perspective may bring temporal meaning to life, but it still does not bring ultimate meaning. If the universe will one day vanish away, what is the ultimate meaning behind anyone's existence?

Following these premises, we arrive at the dreadful conclusion that many great thinkers have already come to: life without

God is meaningless; it is absurd. Renowned atheist philosopher Bertrand Russell summarized this conclusion.

> ... man is the product of causes which had no prevision of the end they were achieving; that his origin, his growth, his hopes and fears, his loves and his beliefs, are but the outcome of accidental collocations of atoms; that no fire, no heroism, no intensity of thought and feeling, can preserve an individual life beyond the grave; that all the labors of the ages, all the devotion, all the inspiration, all the noonday brightness of human genius, are destined to extinction in the vast death of the solar system, and that the whole temple of man's achievement must inevitably be buried beneath the debris of a uni-[4] verse in ruins ...

The legendary writer Ernest Hemingway portrayed this reality in several of his novels. I remember vividly the picture given to us in *The Old Man and the Sea*. In this story Santiago, a seasoned fisherman had fished for days in the gulf with no results. As a result, he lost the respect of the villagers. Finally, he went out farther than usual and, at noon, hooked a huge marlin. For three days Santiago struggled with the huge fish until he finally captured it. However, the fish was too big for the boat and he had to tie the fifteen-hundred-pound beauty to the side of the boat.

Finally he would receive respect as a master fisherman and earn a decent wage for his labor. But as he rowed back to shore, sharks came and ate away at his fish. As the sharks attacked, he courageously fought to keep his prize. However, there were too many attackers and his strength ran out. By the time Santiago returned to shore, there was nothing left of his marlin but a skeleton. After his valiant struggle, Santiago had nothing to show.

---

[4] Bertrand Russel, *Why I am not a Christian* (New York: Simon & Schuster, 1957), p.107

As in life, man rows out to pursue the catch of a meaningful life through work, family, relationships, or whatever he chooses as his fishing ground. One day he seems to catch the big fish, the prize that will bring him purpose, the job he wants, the promotion, the girl of his dreams, financial security, etc. However as he rides with his catch to shore, he realizes that key prize will not survive the sharks of reality. Slowly they eat away at his worth. As Santiago fought to protect his fish, so man fights to protect his dream. But in the end, there are too many sharks and eventually they win. Just as the old man returned to the docks with nothing, so man, after all the efforts of his life, ends up with nothing but a skeleton. He realizes he must live out his existence in a meaningless and hopeless universe doomed for extinction.

Where Am I Going?

As the atheist gazes into the telescope of his future, he sees despair and hopelessness. All that awaits the naturalist is death, extinction for eternity for his universe, for mankind and especially for himself.

As the universe continues to expand, the planets and galaxies will drift farther apart which will cause the universe to use energy and get colder. At some time, the stars will die while matter will collapse, creating black holes. Thus the universe with each passing moment marches toward the arms of death. With this being the inevitable future, we face the reality that we exist in a universe void of hope.

Mankind faces the same outlook. As the universe expands, the planets will be pulled farther away from one another and the earth will no longer be able to sustain life. As the universe faces future extinction, so does mankind. Mankind faces a hopeless future in which our ultimate unavoidable future end is death.

Think of it ... with each minute that passes, each one of us moves one step closer to our own death. According to the atheists, one day, we will cease to exist. Compared to all of time, our life is a spark that flickers for a few moments and disappears forever. What hope can one have when the only sure and permanent reality the future holds for each of us is death?

Thousands of years earlier, King Solomon, the wealthiest king recorded in Bible history, came to the same realization. After turning from God and living for his own pleasure, he realized what life without God looked like.

> I also thought, 'As for men, God tests them so that they may see that they are like the animals. Man's fate is like that of the animals; the same fate awaits them both: As one dies, so dies the other. All have the same breath; man has no advantage over the animal. Everything is meaningless. All go to the same place; all come from dust and to dust all return. (Ecclesiastes 3:18)

When an atheist wrestles with these three questions, "Who am I?", "Why am I here?", and "Where am I going?", he realizes he faces a conclusion that gives no significance to his being, no meaning to his life, and no hope for the future.

The Christian World View

Faith in the existence of an all powerful, all loving God provides radically different conclusions to the three questions all humans must answer. In contrast to the atheist, the Christian can look forward to a life full of significance, meaning and hope. Man is significant because a personal Creator created him. Genesis 1:1 states, "In the beginning, God created the heavens and the earth." God designed a grand and beautiful universe filled with mystery and majesty. He put the stars in place, set the planets in motion, drew every detail on each creature, and sustains the universe in its present order. Genesis 1:27 states, "So God created man in his own image, in the image of God he created him; male and female he created them." The crown jewel of His creation was man and woman. Being created in His image means that we possess an eternal soul, emotions, a will, mental capabilities, and a conscience. A loving God designed us, fashioned our inmost being, and breathed His life-giving spirit into us. He designed us to rule over the rest of creation and to enjoy His love forever. This brings dignity, value, and identity to every human being. All this we receive not because of anything we have done, but simply because of His love for us.

Genesis 1:28 reads, "God blessed them and said to them, 'Be fruitful and increase in number; fill the earth and subdue it. Rule over the fish of the sea and the birds of the air and over every living creature that moves on the ground.' " God created the universe to glorify Himself and for man to enjoy the wonder of His power. God made us to explore, enjoy, and take care of all that He has created but mostly to experience a meaningful relationship with Him for all eternity. God created the universe with a purpose, and man at the center of that plan.

Revelation 22:3 states, "No longer will there be any curse. The throne of God and of the Lamb will be in the city, and His servants will serve Him. They will see His face, and His name will be on their foreheads. There will be no more night. They will not need the light of a lamp or the light of the sun for the Lord God will give them light. And they will reign forever and ever."

According to the Bible, all of creation and history is moving toward a climax when Christ returns to restore creation and rule as king over all. When He rules, He will destroy sin and death and establish an everlasting rule of peace and justice. He has already conquered sin and death through His death on the cross. Those who have received God's gift of forgiveness through His Son Jesus Christ, know God personally and await a glorious eternal future in His presence. Whether physical death takes them into His presence or He returns while they are still here on earth, Christians face a future of eternal hope. Christian song writer, Don Wyrtzen summarizes that hope:

> When surrounded by the blackness of the darkest night O how lonely death can be! At the end of this long tunnel is a shining light for death is swallowed up in victory! But just think of stepping on shore and finding it heaven, of touching a hand and finding it God's, of breathing new air, and finding it celestial, of waking up in glory—and finding it home.

Since man is created by God for an intended reason, he has significance, purpose, and hope. But is this simply wishful thinking or is there proof for the Christian faith? The answer is yes, there is proof! Let's see why there are good reasons for us to believe.

Chapter 2
See the Evidence for God

Can We Prove No God Exists?

I remember one encounter I had with a young man on a university campus who stated emphatically, "I am certain a God does not exist." I responded asking, "Are you absolutely certain of that?" To which he responded in the affirmative. I then stated, "Then you must know all there is to know of the universe. That is incredible!" He looked at me puzzled and said, "Of course not! No one can know all there is to know of the universe." I then stated, "Your statement tells me you know all there is to know of the universe. If you do not have all knowledge of the universe, you cannot make that statement with finality because, in essence, you are stating, 'I have infinite knowledge that no being with infinite knowledge exists.' In other words, 'I know all there is to know about the universe and therefore, I can say beyond the shadow of a doubt, God does not exist.' Allow me to illustrate this point. Suppose I said, 'I am absolutely certain that there are no nails in my house.' To be completely sure of this fact, I would have to search every corner of my house: every room, every floorboard, and every hollow space. Then and only then could I say, 'I am certain there exist no nails in my house.' To say, 'I know for sure God does not exist,' means I have to know all there is to know of the universe to be able to know God does not exist anywhere in the universe. However, how much does man know about the universe? Most cosmologists would tell you man knows less than one percent of all that there is to know. Since man cannot possibly know all there is to know about the universe, he cannot conclusively prove that God does not exist anywhere in the universe. One must entertain the possibility that a God exists. It is impossible to conclusively prove the atheist position."

It is at this point his countenance changed and I was able to show him that all world views, even the atheist position, require a step of faith. The key is to put our faith in what is true. Looking at the evidence, which position is the most reasonably true? Is there a case for theism, or belief in a God?

Where Did the Universe Come From?

The first evidence that there is a God is the existence of the cosmos itself. This is called the cosmological argument. Simply stated, this argument says that if something now exists, it must have (1) come from something else, (2) come from nothing, or (3) have always existed. If it came from something else, that something else must have come from something else, from nothing, or always existed. Ultimately we conclude that if something exists, its origin can be traced to an eternal source, or it originated from nothing.

So what about the universe? We must come to one of three conclusions; either it always existed, it came from nothing, or it came from something else greater than it.

Consider the first conclusion that the universe has always existed. This is the view of pantheist religions ("Pan" from the Greek meaning all, and "theism" meaning God. Eastern religions teach that all that exists in the universe is a part of God.)

Scientific evidence reveals the universe is not eternal but that it had a beginning, the Big Bang. Therefore, the universe itself is not eternal. What then, is the eternal first cause?

The second conclusion is that the universe came from nothing. Little needs to be said since this would be an absurd conclusion. The law of cause and effect—that every cause has an effect and every effect has a cause and no effect is greater than its cause—goes against this possibility. Reason and observation shows nothing produces nothing.

That leads us to consider the third conclusion, that the universe came from a cause greater than itself. That greater cause is an intelligent designer or God. Some ask, where did God come from? God is the uncaused first cause. He is eternal. The Bible states, He is from "Everlasting to everlasting." So what about the Big Bang? God could have used a cataclysmic event in creating the universe. The point here is that it is reasonable to conclude an intelligent designer as a first cause.

It would be most reasonable to conclude that of the three, the most rational explanation is that it came from a cause greater than it. That cause is God.

How Do We Explain the Order and Complexity in Creation?

The second argument for the existence of God is the argument of design or the teleological argument. It is evident that there is complexity and order in the universe. This also suggests the hand of an intelligent designer. If we were walking along the beach and discovered a watch, what would we immediately assume? We would assume someone lost his watch, which was made by a watchmaker. Although all the parts of a watch are found here on this earth, no one in their right mind upon finding the watch would assume, "Wow, what a great feat of evolution! I am amazed at how

Mother Nature created this watch over millions of years." We could even disassemble the watch and leave it on the beach for millions of years but it would never become a watch again. In order to create a watch, an intelligent being must come and assemble the parts into a watch. Order and complexity in the world point to a designer who brings order out of disorder.

If we would not assume the watch evolved by chance, how much more the human body which is a thousand times more complex? The human body is a well-designed machine made up of hundreds of complex systems working in perfect complementary fashion. In a single human chromosome, there is enough information that if printed in book form, it would fill an entire set of encyclopedias. Information from all the DNA in our body could fill multiple libraries. With each movement of my hands, hundreds of neurons and electrical impulses are going back and forth from my brain, down my spine, and to my fingers at thousandths of seconds in perfectly timed sequences. We have yet to create a computer that can do what the human body can do. Could all this be an accident?

Let's look at the planet we live on. The earth has the exact components needed to sustain the delicate balance for life. If the four coupling constants—gravity, strong nuclear, weak nuclear, and electromagnetic—were slightly larger or smaller, the particles, atoms, and molecules necessary for life would not exist, and there would be no sun our size that could support life. If the speed of light were faster or slower, all the fine structure constants would be altered, making life impossible. The earth is the perfect distance from the sun. Any closer and the excess heat would prevent a water cycle. If we were farther away, the cold would do the same. The sun is the right size. Any larger and it would burn too rapidly. If the mass were smaller, the earth would need to be closer, disrupting its rotation. The earth's size allows the right gravitational force needed to create an atmosphere at the right thickness. Water has unique properties to be able to sustain life. While every other liquid freezes and sinks to the bottom, water molecules freeze and expand thus floating to the surface allowing life below the oceans and lakes to survive. More can be said about the exact thickness of the earth's crust, its rotational period, distance from the moon, etc. All these components make the probability of all this happening in such precise order by chance a remote possibility.

To say that such precise order could have come from numerous accidents would be like saying a tornado came through a junkyard and after it blew over, a 747 jumbo jet was created.

As scientists begin to unravel the mysteries of the universe, they find themselves face-to-face with the realization of the apparent design and order of the universe. British astrophysicist Dr. Fred Hoyle states, "A superintellect has monkeyed with physics, as well as chemistry and biology."[5] The more we discover in those and other fields of science, the more we realize the near impossibility of life evolving by mere chance. Physicist Dr. Robert Griffiths who won the Heinemann prize in mathematical physics states, "If we need an atheist to debate, I go to the philosophy department. The physics department isn't much use."[6]

Order and design of the universe points us to the haunting probability of a designer. Astronomer Dr. George Greenstein wrote, "As we survey the evidence, the thought insistently arises that some supernatural agency—or rather, Agency—must be involved. Is it possible that suddenly, without intending to, we have stumbled upon scientific proof of the existence of a Supreme Being?"[7]

The quest of science appears to lead us back to Genesis 1:1, "In the beginning God created the heavens and the earth." NASA scientist and a self-proclaimed agnostic, Dr. Robert Jastrow summed up the circular journey of science. "For the

[5] Fred Hoyle, quoted by Hugh Ross in *The Creator and the Cosmos* (Colorado Springs: NavPress, 1995), p. 121.

[6] Tim Stafford, "Cease-fire in the Laboratory," *Christianity Today*, 3 April 1987, p. 18.

[7] George Greenstein, quoted by Hugh Ross in *The Creator and the Cosmos*, p. 121.

scientist who has lived by faith in the power of reason, the story ends like a bad dream. He has scaled the mountains of ignorance; he is about to conquer the highest peak; as he pulls himself over the final rock, he is greeted by a band of theologians who have been sitting there for centuries."[8]

When you ask an atheist, "How do you explain the apparent order and design in the universe? How did it come to be?" The most common answer I find is, "It just happened. As immense as the odds are, it just happened." To believe that requires a leap of faith. Now let me ask this question, which position requires greater faith? The theist who believes that the cause of the universe is a divine creator or the atheist who proposes that a collision of hydrogen atoms created the universe by accident? The latter requires more faith. I often tell my atheist friends that I admire them for their great faith.

The Moral Argument

Everyone has an innate sense of right and wrong. Even the worst criminals in jail can suffer a sense of guilt for their crime. In fact, we consider those who commit heinous crimes with no sense of guilt functionally insane. All cultures recognize the four universal virtues of honesty, wisdom, courage, and justice. Although they may be expressed in different ways, these four virtues persist in societies around the world. No culture honors a coward who flees from battle. No culture honors a fool.

Whenever a suspect with overwhelming evidence of his guilt gets off free from a trial, people respond with zeal over the sense of injustice they just witnessed. The human soul cannot rest until justice is served. Even little children will argue over issues defending their sense of justice. We often hear them saying, "That's not fair!"

---

[8] Robert Jastrow, *God and the Astronomers* (New York: Norton & Company, 1978), p. 102.

From where do we acquire this sense of right and wrong? The thought of hydrogen evolving into thinking beings with a conscience, will, and ability to reason is inconsistent with scientific observation and philosophical reasoning. A purposeful and moral being cannot arise from impersonal, lifeless matter.

A moral being must come from a creator who is honest, just, courageous, and wise. It is His image we now reflect. Romans 2:14–15 states that our creator instilled within us a conscience that is universal to all men. Being created in the image of God means we reflect the moral qualities of our creator.

Conclusion

I hope that you are willing to entertain the possibility of the existence of an intelligent designer. So far we have shown evidence for the existence of God. We have yet to show what kind of God He is. Has this God communicated to us in any way? Is there proof that He loves His creation and has established a way to have a relationship with Him? The answer is a resounding Yes!

Chapter 3
See the Word of God

*T*here are many books today that claim to be the Word of God. The Koran, which is the Islamic holy book, the Book of Mormon, which is the sacred text of the Mormon Church, and the Bhagavad Gita, which is the most well known of all sacred scriptures from ancient India, are three such examples.

Christians believe the Bible to be the Word of God and the eternal source of truth. Why do Christians think the Bible is the Word of God? Can we prove that the Bible is divinely inspired? I will make the case for divine inspiration by demonstrating that the Bible is unique, true, and supernatural.

The evidence for the authority of the Bible falls into two major categories: internal evidence and external evidence. Internal evidence refers to the evidence that is found within the Bible itself. By external evidence, I mean evidence that is found outside the Bible, such as archaeology, science, philosophy, and ancient manuscripts. Let us first consider the internal evidences.

Internal Evidence

Unity of the Bible

The first evidence is the unity of the Bible. The Bible covers hundreds of topics, yet it does not contradict itself. It remains united in its theme. "What's so amazing about that?" you may ask. Consider these facts. First, the Bible was written over a span of fifteen hundred years.

Second, it was written by more than forty men from every walk of life. For example, Moses was educated in Egypt and became a prophet over Israel, Peter was a simple fisherman, Solomon was a king, Luke was a doctor, Amos was a shepherd, and Matthew was a tax collector. All the writers were of vastly different occupations and backgrounds.

Third, the Bible was written in many different geographical locations. It was written on three different continents: Asia, Africa, and Europe. Moses wrote in the desert of Sinai, Paul wrote in a prison in Rome, Daniel wrote while in exile in Babylon, and Ezra wrote in the ruined city of Jerusalem.

Fourth, it was written under dramatically different circumstances. David wrote during a time of war, Jeremiah wrote at the sorrowful time of Israel's downfall, Peter wrote while Israel was under Roman domination, and Joshua wrote while invading the land of Canaan.

Finally, the writers had different purposes for writing. Isaiah wrote to warn Israel of God's coming judgment on their sin. Matthew wrote to prove to the Jews that Jesus was the Messiah. Zechariah wrote to encourage a disheartened Israel who had returned from Babylonian exile and Paul wrote addressing problems in different Asian and European churches.

Put all these factors together: the Bible was written over fifteen hundred years, by forty different authors, at different places, under various circumstances, and addressing a multitude of issues. It is amazing that with such diversity, the Bible exhibits perfect thematic unity: God's redemption of man and all of creation. Hundreds of controversial subjects are addressed and yet the writers do not contradict each other.

Let me offer you a good illustration. Take just ten medical doctors who graduate from the same medical school in the same year and have them write their viewpoints on five controversial subjects in medicine: euthanasia, abortion, genetic engineering, cloning, and artificial reproduction. Would they all agree on all their points? Certainly not. Now look at the authorship of the Bible. All these authors, over a span of fifteen hundred years, wrote on many controversial subjects, and yet they do not contradict one another on any point.

An objection often raised is, "Didn't a group of men gather at some point, read through several books and determine which would be included in the Bible based on their consistency with one another?" No, the Bible was not created that way. Rather over a two-thousand-year process, books were added to the canon, the collection of works acknowledged as divinely inspired, as they were written by recognized prophets and apostles. The Old Testament was completed in 400 B.C. with the last prophet Malachi. The New Testament canon was in circulation by the second century A.D., but was officially ratified in the early fourth century A.D.

Only after its completion and study did later generations realize the unity of the Bible. The writers had no concrete knowledge of the overall structure. It seems one author guided these writers through the whole process: the Holy Spirit. 1 Peter 2:21 states, "No prophecy was ever made by an act of human will, but men moved by the Holy Spirit spoke from God." There is no book with such diversity of authorship, yet maintaining complete unity in content.

I presented this argument to a professor of literature as we were enjoying a Chinese dinner. After politely listening to my explanation I asked him, "In all your studies, have you ever run across a book like this?" He answered, "If what you are saying is true, I must admit, the Bible is a unique book." I responded, "It is divinely inspired." "No," he responded, "I won't admit that, but I must concede, it is a unique book." The unity of the Bible makes it a book like no other ever written.

Transforming Ability

Second, we have evidence concerning the transforming ability of the Bible. Hebrews 4:12 says, "The word of God is living and active and sharper than any two-edged sword, and piercing as far as the division of soul and spirit." Romans 12:2 says, "And be not conformed to this world but be transformed by the renewing of your mind." The Word of God and the Spirit of God actually transform the lives of people. The Bible has transformed the lives of people from every walk of life: from criminals and drug addicts to government officials, business people, and students. No other book impacts the world like the Bible. This is because the Bible is not a mere book on good living but is literally packed with power. It is the Word of God with the power to change lives.

External Evidence

Now we will study the external evidences of the Bible, that is, evidences found outside the Bible. Indestructibility, archaeology, and prophetic accuracy are three external evidences supporting the Bible.

Indestructibility

The first external evidence is the indestructibility of the Bible. The Bible is the most well-known book in the history of the world, and no book has been attacked more than it. Skeptics have tried to destroy the authority of the Bible for the last eighteen hundred years. It has undergone every kind of scrutiny possible from archaeology, science, philosophy, and computers. Yet, despite all these attacks, the Bible proves itself to be true again and again. Each time the skeptics have been wrong, and the Bible has proven itself true. The poem entitled "The Anvil? God's Word" illustrates this point.

> Last eve I passed beside a blacksmith's door
> and heard the anvil ring the vesper chime:
> then looking in, I saw upon the floor
> old hammers, worn with beating years of time.
> "How many anvils have you had," said I,
> "To wear and batter all these hammers so?"
> "Just one," said he, and then, with twinkling eye,
> "The anvil wears the hammers out, you know."
> And so, thought I, the anvil of God's word,
> for ages skeptic blows have beat upon;
> Yet through the noise of falling blows was heard,
> the anvil is unharmed . . . the hammer's gone.

Just the fact that the Bible has remained steadfast in its authority after two thousand years is another piece of evidence supporting its divine origin.

Archaeology

In studying many religious works, one will see they are filled with myths of gods and demigods performing strange and miraculous feats. Most understand these to be myths and whether they really occurred or not is irrelevant. However, in the Bible, we have a religious book that answers the greatest questions of life and yet it is uniquely a historically accurate book as well. The events it records occurred in the context of history. The veracity of the Bible is upheld by the second source of external evidence, archaeology. Middle Eastern archaeological investigations have proven the Bible to be true and unerringly accurate in its historical descriptions. Nelson Glueck, a renowned Jewish archaeologist, stated, "No archaeological discovery has ever controverted a biblical reference."[9]

Dr. William Albright, who was probably the foremost authority in Middle East archaeology in his time, said this about the Bible: "There can be no doubt that archaeology has confirmed the substantial historicity of the Old Testament."[10] No religious book can compare with the tremendous amount of historical evidence as the Bible. Archaeology proves that the Bible and Christianity is a historical faith based on evidence and it is not just a blind leap in the dark. Here are a few examples:

Archaeology and the Old Testament

The Hittites played a prominent role in Old Testament history. They interacted with biblical figures as early as Abraham (2000 B.C.) and as late as Solomon (1200 B.C.). They are mentioned in Genesis 15:20 as people who inhabited the land of Canaan. In 1 Kings 10:29, they purchased chariots and horses from Solomon. The most prominent Hittite was Uriah the husband of Bathsheba. The Hittites were a powerful force in the Middle East from 1750 B.C. till 1200 B.C. There was no proof of the existence of the Hittites outside the Bible until late in the 19th century. Many critics alleged that this was a fabricated tribe. But in the late 19th and early 20th century, archaeologists began excavating at a city in Turkey named Boghaz-koy. Their search uncovered five temples, a fortified citadel, and several massive

---

9 Nelson Glueck, *Rivers in the Desert: A History of the Negev* (New York: Farrar, Strauss, and Cudahy, 1959), 31.
10 William F. Albright, *Archaeology and the Religion of Israel* (Baltimore: John Hopkins, 1953), 176.

sculptures. In one storeroom over ten thousand clay tablets were discovered. These tablets included treaties, laws, and ceremonial practices. The tablets also named Boghaz-koy as the capital of the Hittite kingdom. Its original name was Hattusha and the city covered an area of 300 acres. The Hittite nation had been discovered!

Linguists soon discovered the Hittite language is an early relative of the Indo-European languages of Greek, Latin, French, German, and English. Now the Hittite language has a central place in the study of the history of the Indo-European languages.

The discovery also confirmed other biblical facts. In the city, five temples were discovered. Written on many tablets were details of the rites and ceremonies the priests performed. The instructions proved to be very elaborate and lengthy. Critics once criticized the laws and instructions found in the books of Leviticus and Deuteronomy as too complicated for the time it was written, 1400 B.C. The Boghaz-koy texts, along with others from Egyptian sites and a site along the Euphrates called Emar, have proven the ceremonies described in the Jewish Pentateuch are consistent with the ceremonies of the cultures of this time period.

Dr. Fred Wright summarized the importance of this find in regard to biblical historicity.

Now the Bible picture of this people fits in perfectly with what we know of the Hittite nation from the monuments. As an empire they never conquered the land of Canaan itself, although the Hittite local tribes did settle there at an early date. Nothing discovered by the excavators has in any way discredited the biblical account. Scripture accuracy has once more been proved by the archaeologist.[11]

---

[11] Fred Wright, *Highlights of Archaeology in the Bible Lands*, (Chicago: Moody Press, 1955), p. 94-95.

Another exciting archaeological find is the city of Jericho. According to the Bible, the conquest of Jericho occurred in approximately 1400 B.C. The miraculous nature of the battle has caused some scholars to dismiss the story as folklore. Even as a Christian, I too was skeptical of this story and others of this nature. Once I researched Jericho, I discovered otherwise.

Over the past century four prominent archaeologists have excavated the site: Carl Watzinger from 1907–1909, John Garstang from 1930–1936, Kathleen Kenyon from 1952–1958, and presently Bryant Wood.

These archaeologists made some fascinating discoveries of the city. First, Jericho did indeed have an impressive fortification system. Surrounding the city was an outer revetment wall fifteen feet high. Atop the revetment wall was an eight-foot mud-brick wall. This wall was fortified by a large earthen rampart on top of which stood another inner-city mud-brick wall. Between the inner-city wall and outer-city wall were domestic structures. This is consistent with Joshua's description of Rahab's dwelling quarters. (Joshua 6) At one section of both walls, large piles of bricks were found at the base indicating a sudden collapse. Many scholars feel an earthquake, which may also explain the damming of the Jordan, caused this. The collapsed bricks formed a ramp for an invader to easily enter the city. (Joshua 6:20)

Of this amazing discovery Garstang stated, "As to the main fact, then, there remains no doubt: the walls fell outwards so completely, the attackers would be able to clamber up and over the ruins of the city." This is remarkable because city walls fall inward, not outward.[12]

A thick layer of soot indicates the city was destroyed by fire as described in Joshua 6:24. Kenyon described it this way. "The destruction was complete. Walls and floors were blackened or reddened by fire and every room was filled with fallen bricks."[13]

---

[12] John Garstang, *The Foundations of Bible History; Joshua, Judges* (London: Constable, 1931), 146.

[13] Kathleen Kenyon and Thomas Holland, *Excavations at Jericho Vol. 3: The Architecture and Stratigraphy of the Tell*, (London: BSA) p. 370.

Archaeologists also discovered large amounts of grain at the site. This is again consistent with the biblical account that the city was captured quickly. If it had fallen as a result of a siege, the grain would have been used up. Also according to 6:17, the Israelites were forbidden to plunder the city but had to destroy it totally. Grain is tremendously valuable for an invading army and it would seem very strange otherwise why the Israelites would not have plundered the grain.

Although the archaeologists agreed Jericho was violently destroyed, they disagreed on the date of the conquest. Garstang held to the biblical date of 1400 B.C. while Watzinger and Kenyon believed the destruction occurred in 1550 B.C. In other words Watzinger and Kenyon believed that when Joshua arrived at Jericho it had been unoccupied for a century. This assertion would pose a serious challenge to the historicity of the Old Testament.

Recent research by Dr. Wood shows otherwise. He discovered that Kenyon's conclusions were based on the absence of imported pottery from Cyprus common in the Late Bronze Age (1550-1400 B.C.) and she ignored the local pottery that was found. Kenyon also excavated in the poorer section of Jericho where one would not expect to find imported pottery.

Wood studied the domestic pottery and discovered it to be 15th century pottery common to the area. Another significant clue was Egyptian amulets shaped in the form of a beetle called scarabs, which were found in the tombs northwest of Jericho. Inscribed under these amulets were the names of Egyptian Pharaohs dating from 1500 to 1386 B.C. showing the cemetery was in use up to the end of the late Bronze Age. Finally a piece of charcoal found in the destruction debris was carbon-14 dated to be 1410 B.C. The evidence led Wood to this conclusion. "The pottery, stratigraphic considerations, scarab data and a carbon-14 date all point to a destruction of the city around the end of the

Late Bronze Age, about 1400 B.C."[14] Archaeology has again confirmed the accuracy of this biblical account.

One of the most beloved characters in the Bible is King David. Scripture says that he was a man after God's own heart. He is revered as the greatest of all Israelite kings and the future messiah, who would bring an everlasting rule of righteousness, is promised to be his descendant. Despite his key role in Israel's history, we had no evidence outside the Bible to attest to his existence until this past decade.

In the summer of 1993, archaeologists made what has been labeled as a phenomenal and stunning discovery. Dr. Avraham Biran and his team of archaeologists were excavating Tell Dan, a mound located in northern Galilee at the foot of Mt. Hermon. The team found an impressive royal plaza and in it they discovered a black basalt stele containing Aramaic inscriptions. A thirteen-line inscription was found but none of the sentences were complete. Some of the lines contained only three letters while the widest contained fourteen letters. The letters that remained were clearly engraved and easy to read.

Line eight read, "The King of Israel." Line nine read "House of David." This is the first reference to King David found outside the Bible. Many critics were forced to reconsider their view on the Israelite king.

In 1994, two more pieces were identified which are connected to this find. The inscriptions refer to Jehoram who was the son of Ahab, ruler over Israel and Ahaziah who was the ruler over the "House of David" or Judah. These names and facts correspond to the account given in 2 Kings 8:7–15 and 9:6–10.

This is another discovery that strongly upholds the accuracy of the Old Testament. Dr. Hershel Shanks of the *Biblical Archaeological Review* magazine stated, "The stele brings to life the biblical text in a very dramatic way. It also gives us more confidence in the historical reality of the biblical text . . ."[15]

---

[14] Bryant Wood, "Did the Israelites Conquer Jericho?" *Biblical Archaeological Review*, March/April, 1990, p. 57.

[15] John Wilford, "Archaeologist say Evidence of House of David Found." *Dallas Morning News*, 6 August 1993, p. 1A.

Another important biblical fact upheld by the discovery is that the kingdoms of Judah and Israel were prominent powers as the Bible describes. Critics long viewed the two nations as simply insignificant states.

Dr. Bryant Wood summarized the importance of this find.

In our day, most scholars, archaeologists and biblical scholars would take a very critical view of the historical accuracy of many of the accounts in the Bible . . . Most scholars today would say that anything prior to the kingdom period is simply folk stories and myths, . . . many times newer discoveries of archaeology have overturned older critical views of the Bible. Many scholars have said there never was a David or a Solomon, and now we have a stele that actually mentions David.[16]

Archaeology and the New Testament

Archaeologists have also discovered numerous facts to confirm the New Testament. Matthew 2 states that Jesus was born during the reign of Herod. Upon hearing that a king had been born, the frightened Herod ordered all children under the age of two to be killed. His slaughter of innocents is consistent with the historical facts that describe his character. Herod was suspicious of anyone whom he thought may take his throne. His list of victims included one of his ten wives, who was his favorite, three of his own sons, a high priest, an ex-king, and two of his sister's husbands. Thus, his brutality portrayed in Matthew is consistent with his description in ancient history.

Luke, who wrote the gospel of Luke and Acts, has proven to be accurate in his accounts. Dr. Norman Geisler stated of Luke, "In all, Luke names thirty-two countries, fifty-four cities and nine islands without any error."[17]

[16] Randall Price, *The Stones Cry Out* (Eugene, OR.: Harvest House Publishers 1997), p. 173.
[17] Norman Geisler, *Baker Encyclopedia of Christian Apologetics*, (Grand Rapids, MI.: Baker Books, 1999), p. 47.

The accuracy of John's gospel has also been attested to by recent discoveries. In John 5:1–15 Jesus heals a man at the Pool of Bethesda. John described the pool as having five porticoes. This site had long been in dispute until recently. Forty feet underground, archaeologists discovered a pool with five porticoes, and the description of the surrounding area matches John's description. In 9:7 John mentioned another long disputed site, the Pool of Siloam. However, this pool was also discovered in 1897, upholding the accuracy of John.

All the gospels give details of the crucifixion of Christ. An important figure mentioned is Pontius Pilate, the governor who presided over the trial of Jesus. Evidence supporting this was discovered in Caesarea Maritama. In 1961, an Italian archaeologist named Antonio Frova uncovered a fragment of a plaque that was used as a section of steps leading to the Caesarea Theater. The inscription, written in Latin, contained the phrase, "Pontius Pilatus, Prefect of Judea has dedicated to the people of Caesarea a temple in honor of Tiberius." This temple is dedicated to the Emperor Tiberius who reigned from 14–37 A.D. This fits well chronologically with the New Testament which records that Pilate ruled as procurator from 26–36 A.D. Tacitus, a Roman historian of the first century, also confirms the New Testament designation of Pilate. He wrote, "Christus, from whom the name had its origin, suffered the extreme penalty during the reign of Tiberius at the hands of one of our procurators, Pontius Pilatus. . . ."

The gospels also give an accurate portrayal of the practice of crucifixion. In 1968, a gravesite in the city of Jerusalem was uncovered containing thirty-five bodies. Each of the men had died a brutal death, which historians believe was the result of their involvement in the Jewish revolt against Rome in 70 A.D. The inscription identified one individual as Yohan Ben Ha'galgol. Studies of the bones performed by osteologists and doctors from the Hadassah Medical School determined the man was twenty-eight years old, stood five feet six inches, and had some slight facial defects due to a cleft right palate.

What intrigued archaeologists were the evidences that this man had been crucified in a manner resembling the crucifixion of Christ. A seven-inch nail had been driven through both feet, which were turned outward so the nail could be hammered inside the Achilles tendon.

Archaeologists also discovered that nails had been driven through his lower forearms. A victim of a crucifixion would have to raise and lower his body in order to breathe. To do this, he needed to push up on his pierced feet and pull up with his arms. Yohan's upper arms were smoothly worn, indicating this movement.

John recorded, that in order to expedite the death of a prisoner, executioners broke the legs of the victim so that he could not lift himself up by pushing with his feet (John 19:31–33). Yohan's legs were found crushed by a blow, breaking them below the knee. The Dead Sea Scrolls, collections of manuscripts found along the Dead Sea dating from the second century B.C. to the second century A.D., tell that both Jews and Romans abhorred crucifixion due to its cruelty and humiliation. The scrolls also state it was a punishment reserved for slaves and any who challenged the ruling powers of Rome. This explains why Pilate chose crucifixion as the penalty for Jesus.

Relating to the crucifixion, in 1878 a stone slab was found in Nazareth with a decree from Emperor Claudius who reigned from 41–54 A.D. It stated that graves must not be disturbed nor bodies removed. The punishment on other decrees is a fine, but this one threatens death and comes very close to the time of the resurrection. This was probably due to Claudius investigating the riots of 49 A.D. He had certainly heard of the resurrection and did not want any similar incidents. This decree was probably made in connection with the Apostles' preaching of Jesus' resurrection and the Jewish argument that the body had been stolen.

These are some convincing archaeological findings authenticating the historical reliability of the Bible. Hundreds of discoveries further confirm its historicity. No book is as ancient, and at the same time, as convincingly accurate as the Bible. Since archaeology has confirmed numerous Bible accounts, we can safely conclude that it is trustworthy and that all of its accounts are true. Indestructibility and archaeology are two external evidences for the Bible.

Prophetic Accuracy

There are many more external evidences for the Bible, but I'll just cover one more: evidence from prophecy. The record of prophecy best attests to the supernatural nature of the Bible. The Bible contains hundreds of fulfilled prophecies. No book in history compares to its accuracy.

One of the most respected prophets is Nostradamus, who lived in the sixteenth century A.D., and many have claimed that hundreds of his prophecies have come true. However, many have not come to pass. If you read his prophecies, you will find them to be vague and unclear. His symbols and language can be taken to mean a number of historical events. Here is one of the most famous examples used, the prophecy of Hitler.

> In the year that is to come soon, and not far from
> Venus, the two greatest ones of Asia and Africa, shall be
> said to come from the Rhine and Ister, crying and tears
> shall be at Malta and on the Italian shore.[18]

---

[18] Ray Comfort, *The Secrets of Nostradamus Exposed* (Bellflower, CA.: Living Waters, 1996), p. 47.

Ister is attributed to denote Hitler. However, the context makes it clear Ister is not a man but a river.

Unlike this type of prophecy, biblical prophecy is clear, specific and must be totally correct. According to Deuteronomy 18:20–22, a prophet's predictions must come true one hundred percent of the time.

I was speaking with a coworker once who happened to be Jewish and an atheist. She went through several arguments to defend her world view and concluded with this statement. She said, "I am Jewish. I have grown up in the traditions of Judaism since I was a child. If anyone should believe in God, it should be me for I was reared in a culture that honors the Old Testament. The fact that I am Jewish and have become an atheist is convincing proof of atheism." I asked her, "Are you sure you are Jewish?" To that she abruptly scoffed and said, "Of course I am. I can trace my heritage back to several centuries." I then replied, "Then you are living proof of biblical prophecy." Surprised at my response I shared with her the Jeremiah prophecy. This got her attention and allowed me to share my position and she listened intently. Jeremiah 31:35–36 states,

> This is what the Lord says, he who appoints the sun to shine by day, who decrees the moon and stars to shine by night, who stirs up the sea so that its waves roar–the Lord Almighty is His name: Only if these decrees vanish from my sight, declares the Lord, will the descendants of Israel ever cease to be a nation before me.

In other words, the people of Israel will not cease to be a nation until the Lord returns. Imagine telling the ruler of the golden Babylonian Empire, this little nation of Israel, whose capital city you destroyed and the people you deported, will long outlive your Empire. One day the Babylonian Empire will cease, but Israel will live on. I am sure the king would have laughed at this thought. Imagine telling the Emperor of Rome that the tiny nation of Israel would long outlive the powerful Roman Empire. You would have met the same skepticism. Empires have risen and fallen but Israel remains. The fact this nation has remained for four thousand years is a testimony to Bible prophecy.

Ezekiel 26 is another grand testimony to the greatness of Bible prophecy. In fact you can travel to Lebanon today and see the remains of this prophetic fulfillment. The prophecy reads as follows:

> I am against you O Tyre, and I will bring many nations against you, like the sea casting up its waves. They will destroy the walls of Tyre and pull down her towers; I will scrape away her rubble and make her a bare rock. Out in the sea she will become a place to spread fishnets, for I have spoken, declares the sovereign Lord." It further states, "They will plunder your wealth and loot your merchandise; they will break down your walls and demolish your fine houses and throw your stones, timber and rubble into the sea. (Ezekiel 26:3–6, 12)

Written in 587 B.C., Ezekiel prophesied that the mighty city of Tyre would be destroyed. Tyre was made up of two parts, a mainland port city and an island city half a mile offshore. Ezekiel predicted mainland Tyre would be destroyed by Nebuchadnezzar, many nations would fight against her, the debris of the city would be thrown into the ocean, the city would never be found again, and fishermen would come there to lay their nets.

In 573 B.C., Nebuchadnezzar destroyed the mainland city of Tyre. Many of the refugees sailed to the island which remained a powerful city. In 333 B.C., however, Alexander the Great laid siege to Tyre. Using the rubble of mainland Tyre, he built a causeway to the island city of Tyre. He then captured and completely destroyed the city.

Today, Tyre is a small fishing town where fishing boats come to rest and fishermen spread their nets. The great ancient city of Tyre to this day lies buried in ruins exactly as prophesied. If we were to calculate the odds of this event happening by chance, the figures would be astronomical. No, it was not by coincidence.[19]

Here's another example. There are over one hundred prophecies made about Jesus in the Old Testament, such as His place of birth, how He would die, His rejection by the nation of Israel, and so on. All these prophecies were made hundreds of years before Jesus ever came to earth. Because of the accuracy of the prophecies, many skeptics have believed that they must have been written after 70 A.D.—after the birth and death of Jesus, and the destruction of Jerusalem. Critics have tried to deny that they even are prophecies.

However, in 1947, the Dead Sea Scrolls were discovered. These scrolls contained the book of Isaiah and other prophetic books. When dated, they were found to be written from 120 to 100 B.C., well before Jesus was born.[20] It would have been an incredible accomplishment for Jesus to have fulfilled all these prophecies. Some say these prophecies were fulfilled by chance, but the odds for this would be exceptionally large. It would take more faith to believe in that chance happening than in the fact that Jesus is God and these prophecies are divinely inspired.

---

[19] Ralph H. Alexander, "Ezekiel," in *The Expositor's Bible Commentary*, ed. Frank E. Gaebelein (Grand Rapids: Zondervan, 1986), 869.

[20] Norman Geisler, *A General Introduction to the Bible* (Chicago: Moody Press, 1986), p. 365-366.

No book can match the Bible when it comes to prophecy. The prophetic record proves the supernatural nature of the Bible. Its testimony points us to the author who is eternal and has infinite knowledge even over the future.

Chapter 4
See an Accurate Copy

I have made a defense for the divine inspiration of the Bible. Since God inspired the original writers, the original documents contain no errors. This is called the doctrine of inerrancy. Divine inspiration and the doctrine of inerrancy applies only to the original texts, not the copies. Therefore, we must now address the challenge: how true to the originals is our Bible? We do not possess the original documents of Paul, John, or Moses. How then do we know that our present day Bible is a well-preserved and accurate copy of their work? Several other belief systems like liberal denominations, Muslims, and Mormons, just to name a few, allege that the present-day Bible cannot be trusted since it has been altered over the years and that it contains numerous copyist errors.

When I was in college, a professor of history posed this challenge to me. He stated, "What we have are copies of the originals. Since there were no Xerox machines, computers, or video cameras, how can we expect the Bible to have been transmitted to us accurately? Even with all our technology, we still make a considerable amount of errors." The answer to this challenge leads us into the fascinating study called textual criticism. Textual criticism is the study of ancient texts to determine how accurate present-day translations are to the original text.

What we will discover is that the Bible is ninety-seven percent accurate to the original text. The three percent of the text in dispute are minor and in no way affects any major theological issues. We can be assured that our present-day Bible is a tremendously accurate copy.

The Originals

1 Peter 1:21 states, "For prophecy never had its origin in the will of man, but men spoke from God as they were carried along by the Holy Spirit." In other words, when the prophets and apostles wrote Scripture, they were guided by God the Holy Spirit. What they wrote was a manuscript without error. (Proof of divine inspiration is explained in the previous chapter.)

Yet, we do not have the original writings. Instead what we have are copies of copies of copies handed down from generation to generation. The scribes who copied the text by hand wrote the copies and passed them along for others to copy and distribute.

The copies were extremely accurate but over time errors were made. Some were errors of the eye. In some cases manuscripts arrived and some of the words were difficult to read. The translator then wrote in what he thought the original word was, and on some occasions he was incorrect. At other times, a scribe missed a word or a letter or even an entire sentence. At other times, a scribe would read a manuscript and, believing the previous scribe to be in error, add in a word or sentence that he felt was missing.

Despite these errors, the copies remained very accurate. Were these errors corrected and have we been able to improve the accuracy over the years? The answer is yes.

Finding and Correcting

The science of textual criticism seeks to decipher copyist errors and bring the text closer to the original. In this process scholars find ancient manuscripts and match them up side by side. As they do, they discover where the differences are and can easily discover and correct errors. For example, if I have fifty students hand copy an article from a newspaper, I can count on the fact that some students will make an error in copying. If I match each student's copy side by side and look at the copies, I can easily discover where the errors are. If two students write, "The thief hit the cashier and injured him," but the forty-seven other students wrote, "The thief tried to hit the cashier and missed injuring him," I immediately know one group is wrong. Most likely the forty-seven students are right and the two are wrong. We can easily conclude this since it is far less likely for forty-seven students to be wrong than two would be. Unless there is compelling evidence, this is the most logical assumption.

This is an example of the art of textual criticism. Scholars take the hundreds of copies they have and compare them to one another. When differences are found, they can see where they are, derive the source of the error, and make the correction. The accuracy of this process depends on the number of ancient manuscripts we have and how timely they are to the life of the author. These are the two key elements. Let me illustrate using the same example. If I asked two students to make handwritten copies of the newspaper article, I may get a pretty accurate copy. However, if I asked fifty students to make handwritten copies and then compare their work to check for errors, I would get a much more accurate copy. Suppose I asked one hundred students. The copy would be very accurate if not exact. In other words the more copies I have to compare, the greater the accuracy.

Following the same example, suppose I ask one student to make a handwritten copy of a newspaper article and then pass his copy to the next student one month later and ask the following students to do the same and we end at the fiftieth student. Now which copy would be more accurate to the original, the copy from the fifth student in line or the copy from the forty-ninth student in line? Of course the one from the fifth student in line since his copy is closer in time to the original. The same is true in textual criticism. Not only is the amount of manuscripts critical, how close they are in date to the author's life is key as well in determining accuracy.

Testing the Bible

The New Testament

Let us put this test on the Bible. The first key in determining accuracy is the number of manuscripts. When it comes to the New Testament, we have over 24,000 ancient New Testament manuscripts dating from the second century A.D. to the eighth century A.D. We can therefore derive an accurate text very close to the original since we have thousands of texts to compare. As we examine the texts, we can find the errors and decipher what the original structure is.

How do other ancient texts of history compare with the Bible? Let us take a look at a few and compare. Much of what we know about the Greek and Roman Empire come from the texts of Josephus, Tacitus, Pliny, Thucydides, and Homer. Although we do not have their original texts, we have what historians conclude are very accurate copies of the originals. How many ancient manuscripts are there in some of these best-attested-to works?

Plato's work *Tetralogies* has seven manuscripts. No one doubts the accuracy of Julius Caesar's *Gallic Wars*, but we possess only ten copies from ancient manuscripts. Twenty copies uphold the *Annals* of Tacitus. By far the most well-attested work is the *Iliad* by Homer. The accuracy of this work is derived from 643 manuscripts. These works are considered historically accurate but they fall far short in terms of manuscript number when compared to the New Testament.

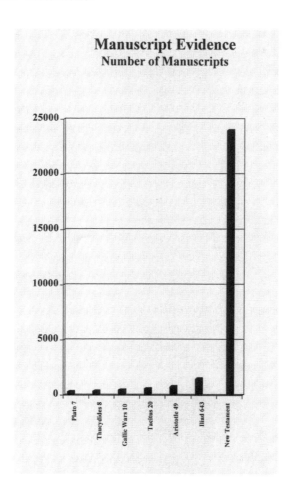

Manuscript Evidence
Number of Manuscripts

Let us apply the time factor to the New Testament. The New Testament was written anywhere from 50–100 A.D. We have manuscripts dating from 1400 A.D. and as early as 114 A.D. The earliest complete New Testament is dated 250 A.D. From the date of writing to the oldest manuscript available, there is a lapse of about fifty years. There is about a two-hundred-year gap to the oldest completed copy of the New Testament. Let's compare that to the works cited earlier. The earliest manuscript copy of Plato is 900 A.D. There is a lapse of 1300 years between the date of writing and the earliest manuscript. With Caesar's *Gallic Wars*, written in 52 B.C., the oldest manuscript we have is dated 900 A.D. showing a 1000-year lapse. The *Annals* of Tacitus is written in 100 B.C. and the oldest manuscript copy dates 850 A.D. revealing an 800-year lapse. How about the best-attested-to Greek work, the *Iliad*? The date of writing is 900 B.C. but the earliest copy we have is 400 B.C., showing a 500-year gap. What we discover is that the New Testament is far superior to any work written during its time. If historians consider the works of Plato and Homer accurate, they must uphold the accuracy of the New Testament or deny all we know of the Greek and Roman Empire as inaccurate and unreliable. For the New Testament surpasses them in its textual evidence.

Work	When Written	Earliest Copy	Time Span
Plato	427 – 447 BC	900 AD	1,200 yrs
Thucydides	460 – 400 BC	900 AD	1,300 yrs
Gallic Wars	100 – 44 BC	900 AD	1,000 yrs
Tacitus	100 AD	1100 AD	1,000 yrs
Aristotle	384 BC	1100 AD	1400 yrs
Iliad	900 BC	400 BC	500 yrs
New Testament	50-100 AD	125 AD	25 yrs

Date of manuscripts

The Old Testament

The Old Testament does not have the abundance of manuscript evidence as the New Testament. It was not possible to preserve the law on animal skins for 4,000 years. All worn-out copies were ceremonially buried. Furthermore, scribes who standardized the Hebrew canon in the fifth century destroyed all the copies they felt were not accurate. What remained were a few copies dating about 900 A.D. Our current Hebrew text from which we derive the present-day Old Testament is called the Masoretic Text.

However, the evidence indicates our present text is accurate to the original. Jewish traditions and laws regarding the copying process reveal that the Israelites had a profound reverence for the Old Testament. They understood they were copying God's sacred law and as a result, were very precise and careful in the process. The Jewish law guided every meticulous aspect from the materials used, to counting the number of lines, columns, and even letters on a page to ensure accuracy. There was even a ceremony performed each time the Lord's name was written. But the true test of accuracy came in 1949.

A shepherd boy looking for his lost sheep discovered caves along the Dead Sea in Israel and threw a rock in to scare the animal. Instead of hearing an animal's cry, he heard a pot crack. Upon entering the cave, he discovered large jars containing sacred scrolls. He had accidentally made one of the greatest discoveries of the century, now known as the Dead Sea Scrolls. The scrolls contained the entire book of Isaiah along with thousands of fragments representing every book of the Bible. From the evidence, scholars have dated the scrolls to be from the third century B.C. to the first century A.D. The oldest copy of the Old Testament is dated 900 A.D. With this discovery, the accuracy of the copying process could be tested since a document written one thousand years before the present-day text had now surfaced. If there was a great deal of variation, it would show that the transmission process was inaccurate.

The comparison of the two revealed some amazing results. The Dead Sea Scrolls and the present-day text were remarkably similar. For example, the two copies of the book of Isaiah were identical to over ninety-five percent of the present text. Slight variations were the result of slips of the pen or spelling. The discovery has confirmed the faith of Christians everywhere because it displayed that over a thousand-year period, the transmission process was indeed very exact and that very little change to the text had occurred. It also discredited those who claimed the Bible had been altered over the years.

It can be concluded from the evidence that the present-day Bibles are accurate to the originals and have not been altered. The minute differences between the texts do not affect or change the meaning of any major doctrine.

Chapter 5
See God in the Flesh

God wrote His Word for us, which is the Bible. It is one way He revealed Himself to us. But He has also revealed Himself personally. God the Son came to earth. The Word became flesh. It was during His time on earth that He also provided the way to have a personal relationship with Him.

Jesus, A Person of History

It is important to establish the fact that Jesus Christ was a historical figure and not a legend. There are several highly accurate historical documents that attest to Jesus. First, let's look at the four gospels themselves. The authors, Matthew, Mark, Luke, and John, recorded very specific details surrounding the life of Jesus, and archaeology has verified most of them. Hundreds of facts such as the names of officials, geographical sites, financial currencies, and times of events have been validated.

The textual evidence decisively shows that the gospels were written and circulated during the lifetime of those who witnessed the events. Since there are so many specific names and places mentioned, the eyewitnesses could have easily discredited incorrect information within the writings. The New Testament never would have survived had the facts been wrong. These facts indicate that the gospels are historically reliable and show Jesus to be a historical figure.

There are several historical works, both Jewish and Roman, that verify Jesus' historicity. One such work is the writings of Josephus. (37 A.D.–100 A.D.) Much of what we know of the Roman Empire and its activities in the first and second century in Palestine come from the works of Josephus. He recorded Antiquities, a history of the Jews, for the Romans during 70 A.D.–100 A.D.

He made a very interesting reference to Jesus.

> Now there was about that time Jesus, a wise man, if it be lawful to call him a man, for he was a doer of wonderful works, a teacher of such men as receive the truth with pleasure. He drew over to him both many of the Jews and many of the gentiles. He was the Christ and when Pilate, at the suggestion of the principal men amongst us, had condemned him to the cross, those that loved him at first did not forsake him. For he appeared alive again the third day, as the divine prophets had foretold these and ten thousand other wonderful things concerning him; and the tribe of Christians, so named from him, are not extinct to this day.[21]

In this paragraph, Josephus not only mentioned Christ but also summarized His life as presented in the gospels.

An important Roman historian is Tacitus. In 115 A.D. he recorded Nero's persecution of the Christians.

> Christus, from whom the name had its origin, suffered the extreme penalty during the reign of Tiberius at the hands of one of our procurators, Pontius Pilatus, and a most mischievous superstition, thus checked for the moment, again broke out not only in Judea,...but even in Rome.[22]

[21] Josephus, *Antiquities* xviii. 33. (Early second century.)
[22] Tactius, *Annals*, 15.44

Tacitus named Christ, Pontius Pilate, and the events surrounding the crucifixion. There are over thirty-nine sources outside the New Testament that attest to over one hundred facts regarding the life and teachings of Jesus. Even if we did not have the gospels, we could still reconstruct the life of Christ from these other writings.

Liar, Lunatic, or Lord?

A study of the gospels leads a person to one of three conclusions about Jesus. Either He was (1) an evil lying villain, (2) a preposterously deluded lunatic, or (3) the Lord Himself, the Son of God. It is ludicrous for anyone who has studied His life to take the position that He was simply a good teacher because of what He said and believed about His identity. Thus, only one of the three conclusions is a logical possibility.

Jesus made some outrageous claims that no ordinary person would dare make. First, He claimed to be God. His statements of equality with God meant He believed that He possessed the authority, attributes, and adoration that belongs only to God. He proclaimed authority over creation, forgiveness of sins, and life and death. He declared to possess the attributes of God. He emphatically stated that He was the source of truth and the only way to eternal life. Of all the significant leaders of history, only Jesus made such claims.

Here are a few of His outrageous claims. When His disciple Philip said, " 'Lord, show us the Father.' Jesus answered. . . . 'Anyone who has seen me has seen the Father.' " (John 14:8–9) Once, when the Pharisees were disparaging and challenging Jesus, He responded, " 'I and the Father are one.' Again the Jews picked up stones to stone Him, but Jesus said to them, 'I have shown you many great miracles from the Father. For which of these do you stone Me?' 'We are not stoning You for any of these,' replied the Jews, 'but for blasphemy, because You, a mere man, claim to be God.' " (John 10:30–33) It is clear in these two statements, Jesus claimed to be God. His opponents clearly understood His declaration of equality with God.

When challenged by the scholars on His authority over Abraham, the father of the Jews, Jesus replied, " 'Your father Abraham rejoiced at the thought of seeing My day; he saw it and was glad.' The Jews said to Him, 'You are not yet fifty years old, and you have seen Abraham!' 'I tell you the truth,' Jesus answered, 'before Abraham was born, I am!' " (John 8:56–58). Jesus clearly believed He had existed two thousand years earlier and knew Abraham.

On the issue of life and death Jesus stated, "I am the resurrection and the life. He who believes in Me will live, even though he dies." (John 11:25) Jesus believed He had authority over life and death.

Finally, Jesus accepted and encouraged others to worship Him. Throughout the gospels the disciples worshipped Jesus as seen in Matthew 14:33 and John 9:38. Jesus stated in John 5:22–23, "Moreover, the Father judges no one but has entrusted all judgment to the Son, that all may honor the Son just as they honor the Father. He who does not honor the Son does not honor the Father, who sent Him." Jesus knew the Old Testament command "Worship the Lord your God, and serve Him only." (Matthew 4:10) Despite this, Jesus received worship. Either He had an overactive imagination or He was who He claimed to be and deserved to be worshiped as God incarnate.

The teachings regarding the deity of Christ were clearly taught in the gospels as well as in the core of early church teaching. Pliny the Younger, Emperor of the Roman province of Bythynia in northwestern Turkey, wrote to Emperor Trajan in 112 A.D.:

> They were in the habit of meeting on a certain fixed day
> before it was light, when they sang an anthem to Christ
> as God, and bound themselves by a solemn oath not to
> commit any wicked deed, but to abstain from all fraud,
> theft and adultery, never to break their word, or deny a
> trust when called upon to honor it; after which it was
> their custom to separate, and then meet again to partake
> of food, but ordinary and innocent kind.[23]

Here Pliny affirmed the fact that the church worshipped
Christ as God. This teaching was not a legend that developed
generations after Jesus' death but was taught from the beginning
of the church.

Imagine if you appeared on a late-night talk show and
said, "I am God, the creator and sustainer of the universe." Later
you stated, "George Washington was glad to see me in his day. He
saw me and he was glad." Imagine the look on the face of the host
as you seriously made such claims. I suppose you would not be a
return guest any time in the near future.

Imagine you walked on the stage of the First Baptist
Church, grabbed the mike and said, "Our next hymn is number
167, 'Immortal Invisible.' This is a hymn about me. As you sing
this, know I am here to accept your praise and worship." It's likely you would be escorted out and taken to the nearest mental
clinic. However, these are the types of outrageous claims Jesus
made. A man making claims like these must either be a diaboli-
cal liar, insane, or truly God incarnate. For the remainder of this
chapter we will be discussing which of these conclusions is most
plausible.

---

[23] Pliny the Younger, Epistles X:96

A Liar?

We have established at this point that Jesus made some astounding claims about Himself. He presumed to be God, claimed the authority and attributes of God, and encouraged others to worship Him as God. If Jesus was a liar, then He knew His message was false but was willing to deceive thousands with claims He knew were untrue. That is, Jesus knew that He was not God, He did not know the way to eternal life, and He died and sent thousands to their deaths for a message He knew was a lie. This would make Jesus history's greatest villain (and perhaps, a demon) for teaching this wicked lie. He would have also been history's greatest fool for it was these claims that led Him to His own death.

Few, if any, seriously hold to this position. Even the skeptics unanimously agree that He was at least a great moral teacher. William Lecky, one of Britain's most respected historians and an opponent of Christianity wrote, "It was reserved for Christianity to present the world an ideal character which through all the changes of eighteen centuries has inspired the hearts of men with an impassioned love."[24]

However, it would be inconsistent and illogical to believe that Jesus was a great moral teacher if some of those teachings contained immoral lies about himself. He would have to be a stupendous hypocrite to teach others honesty and virtue and all the while preach the lie that He was God. It is inconceivable to think that such deceitful, selfish, and depraved acts could have issued forth from the same being who otherwise maintained from the beginning to the end of His life the purest and noblest character known in history.

---

[24] William Lecky, *History of European Morals from Augustus to Charlemagne* (New York: D. Appleton and Company, 1903), p. 8.

A Lunatic?

Since the liar conclusion is not logical, let us assume He really believed He was God but was mistaken. If He truly believed He had created the world, had seen Abraham two thousand years before, and had authority over death, and yet none of this was true, we can only conclude that He was insane.

However, when you study the life of Jesus, He clearly did not display the characteristics of insanity. The abnormalities and imbalances we find in a deranged person are not there. His teachings, such as the Sermon on the Mount, remain among the greatest works ever recorded. The Pharisees and lawyers, highly educated men whose modern day equivalent would be our university professors, continually challenged Jesus. They were fluent in several languages and were known for their scholarship of the Old Testament and Jewish law. They challenged Jesus with some of the most profound questions of their day and Jesus' quick answers amazed and silenced them. In the face of tremendous pressure, we find He exemplified the greatest composure.

The best examples are found in the Gospel of Matthew chapter 22. Here Jesus faced some of the very difficult trick questions that were meant to entrap him. In Matthew 22:15–22, the Pharisees asked Jesus, "Tell us then, what is your opinion? Is it right to pay taxes to Caesar or not?" In this situation, Jesus was set up in a fatal predicament. If He said, "No, do not pay taxes," He would be liable for treason against the Roman government. If He said, "Yes, pay taxes," He would be accused of betraying the nation of Israel. Their cleverly devised question had no winning answer.

Knowing He was being set up, Jesus rebuked them, "'Show me the coin used for paying the tax.' They brought Him a denarius, and He asked them, 'Whose portrait is this? And whose inscription?' 'Caesar's,' they replied. Then He said to them, 'Give to Caesar what is Caesar's, and to God what is God's.' " He answered their unanswerable question with such insight, Scripture states, "When they heard this, they were amazed."

On another occasion, the Sadducees came to question Jesus. The Sadducees were the priests who served at the temple of Jerusalem, the most sacred site for the Jewish people. Many of the Sadducees also held important government positions. They wanted to ask Jesus a question that had never been solved. Since the Sadducees did not believe in a resurrection after death, they asked what had stumped the greatest minds for centuries. In Matthew 22:23-33, they told a story of a woman who married a man who soon afterward died. She then married the man's brothers who all for some reason died of an illness. After being a wife of seven brothers, whose wife would she be in the resurrection of the dead?

Jesus displayed his sound mind and keen wisdom in His response. He said, "You are in error because you do not know the Scriptures or the power of God. At the resurrection people will neither marry nor be given in marriage; they will be like the angels in heaven." So He answered the marriage question and further displayed His genius in the second part of His answer. He revealed the Sadducees' error of not believing in the resurrection from the dead. Since they only believed the first five books of the Old Testament were authoritative, Jesus pointed them to the second book of the Old Testament, Exodus 3:6 when God said, "I am the God of Abraham, Isaac, and Jacob." If the Sadducees were correct, then Abraham, Isaac, and Jacob died two thousand years ago and would no longer exist. God should have said, "I was the God of . . ." Instead, God stated, "I am the God of ..." because He was still their God. In other words, they were still alive in a spiritual state even after physical death.

In both instances, as well as on many other occasions, Jesus answered the most profound questions of His day quickly, authoritatively, and with insight never seen before. For these reasons, the lunatic argument is not consistent.

The Lord?

Thus far we have learned that Jesus is unique among all men for the profound statements He made about His divinity. It is impossible to state He was simply a good moral teacher. From His amazing statements, our only choices are that He must be a liar, a lunatic, or God. Since the first two are not conceivable, we will begin looking at the third alternative—that He really is God. First, we must see if He had the credentials for these claims.

Prophecy

One of the most convincing types of evidence is the testimony of prophecy. The Old Testament contains a number of messianic prophecies made centuries before Christ appeared on the earth. The fact that He fulfilled each one is powerful evidence that He was no ordinary man. Allow me to illustrate this point using eight prophecies.

1. Genesis 12:1–3 states the Messiah would come from the seed of Abraham.
2. Genesis 49:10 states that He would be of the tribe of Judah.
3. 2 Samuel 7:12 states that Messiah would be of the line of King David.
4. Micah 5:2 states that He would be born in the city of Bethlehem.

5. Daniel 9:24 states He would die or be "cut off" exactly 483 years after the declaration to reconstruct the temple in 444 B.C.
6. Isaiah 53 states that the Messiah would die with thieves, then be buried in a rich man's tomb.
7. Psalm 22:16 states upon His death, His hands and His feet would be pierced. This is quite significant since Roman crucifixion had not been invented at the time the psalmist wrote.
8. Isaiah 49:7 states that Messiah would be known and hated by the entire nation. Not many men become known by their entire nation, and even less are despised by the entire nation.

Now calculate the possibility of someone fulfilling these prophecies by coincidence. Let us suppose you estimate there is a one in one hundred chance a man could fulfill just one of these prophecies by chance. That would mean when all eight are put together there is a 1/10 to the 16th power probability that they were fulfilled by chance. Mathematician Peter Stoner estimated 1/10 to the seventeenth power possibility that these prophecies were fulfilled by chance.[25] Mathematicians have estimated that the possibility of sixteen of these prophecies being fulfilled by chance is about 1/10 to the 45th power.[26] That's a decimal point followed by 44 zeroes and a 1! These figures show it is extremely improbable that these prophecies could have been fulfilled by accident. The fact is, Jesus fulfilled not just eight or sixteen prophecies, He fulfilled 109 major prophecies.[27]

Skeptics have objected to the testimony of prophecy, stating they were written after the time of Jesus and therefore fulfill themselves. However, the evidence overwhelmingly shows these prophecies were clearly written centuries before Christ. The Old

[25] Josh McDowell, *Evidence That Demands a Verdict* (San Bernadino, Calif.: Here's Life Publishers, 1979), p. 167.

[26] Norman Geisler, *When Skeptics Ask* (Wheaton, Ill.: Victor Press, 1990), p. 116.

[27] Tim LaHaye, *Jesus, Who is He?* (Sisters, Ore.: Multnomah Books, 1996), p. 176.

Testament canon was completed by 400 B.C. The Septuagint, the Greek translation of the Old Testament, was completed in the reign of Ptolemy Philadelphus in 250 B.C. The Dead Sea Scrolls discovered in 1948 contained the books of the Old Testament. Prophetic books like Isaiah were dated by paleographers to be written in 100 B.C.[28] Once again, these prophecies were confirmed to be written centuries before Christ. No religious leader has even come close to fulfilling the number of prophecies Jesus has fulfilled.

If a person claimed to be God, we would expect supernatural confirmations. We have already discovered the phenomenal record of prophecy. We would also expect Him to demonstrate authority over truth, nature, sickness, sin, and death. Jesus did demonstrate such authority.

Command Over Truth

Jesus' teachings displayed His command of truth. Although not formally educated, Jesus was able to teach God's Word with such insight He astounded the scholars. For example, the Sermon on the Mount is still viewed as one of the greatest and most beautiful religious discourses ever recorded. Jesus' teachings have had a profound impact on every facet of human civilization: government, legal systems, marriage, medical ethics, literature, music, and education even to this day.

Miracles

The next line of evidence is seen in His miraculous deeds. Jesus' miracles demonstrated His power over creation, sickness, and death. He showed His authority over nature in such miracles as walking on water (Matthew 14:25), multiplying bread (Matthew

---

28 Norman Geisler and William Nix, *A General Introduction to the Bible* (Chicago: Moody Press, 1986), pp. 365–66.

14:15-21), and calming the storm (Mark 4:35–41). He ruled over sickness with His healings of terminal diseases. These healings did not take weeks or days but were complete and instantaneous. He healed blindness (John 9), paralysis (Mark 2), leprosy (Luke 17), and deafness (Mark 7). Such miracles cannot be attributed to psychosomatic healing but to one who rules over creation. Jesus displayed authority over death by raising the dead as recorded in Luke 7 and Matthew 9.

Some doubt whether these miracles occurred. Several view the miracle accounts as fictitious legends developed after the death of Christ. Philosopher David Hume argued that human nature tends to gossip and exaggerate the truth. Others say that the miracle accounts were propagated in distant lands by the followers of Christ well after the actual events so that the miracle accounts could not have been verified due to distance and time.

There are several arguments against these attacks. First, the Bible has proven to be a historically reliable document. Second, legends and exaggerations develop when followers travel to distant lands well after the time of the events and tell of stories which cannot be confirmed. Legends usually develop generations after the death of the figure, at which time it is impossible to verify any of the accounts since witnesses may not be available. However, the accounts of Jesus' miracles were told in the very cities in which they occurred during the lifetime of Jesus and to those who witnessed the events. Those who saw the miracles were both followers of Christ as well as His enemies. These eyewitnesses were questioned carefully by those in authority. If any claims were exaggerated or distorted, they could have easily been refuted. The New Testament miracle accounts could not have survived had the accounts been false.

German scholar Dr. Carsten Theide and British scholar Dr. Matthew D'Ancona, in their book *Eyewitness to Jesus*, stated their conclusions after scientifically investigating a fragment from the Gospel of Matthew. This evidence revealed that Matthew was written before 70 A.D.[29] This finding proved the fact that Matthew, and very likely the other gospels, was written and circulated during the lifetime of eyewitnesses, who were able to verify the accuracy of such accounts, as well as others, who were unable to refute the accounts of Jesus' miracles. No religious leader has performed miracles as Jesus did.

Clearly the record of prophecy proved there was something unique about Him. The miracles He performed remain unequaled by anyone. But Jesus' greatest demonstration of authority is revealed in His power over sin and death.

Authority Over the Grave

There are many religions and religious leaders who claim to know what lies beyond the grave. The problem is, no one has demonstrated authority over the grave or confirmed their belief of what happens after death. Only Jesus demonstrated authority over death. All men have died, but Jesus is alive.

During His three-year ministry, Jesus exercised His authority by raising several people from the grave. Most notable is the account of Lazarus found in John 11. Even under the watchful eyes of His enemies, Jesus raised Lazarus from the grave. If this were not a historical account, this story would not have survived since it was recorded and propagated in the very city where it occurred, in the lifetime of the witnesses who were both followers and enemies of Christ. The enemies of Christianity could have easily refuted the account if it were not true. The fact is they could not disprove it.

The Old Testament predicted the death of the Messiah in Psalm 22 and Isaiah 53. However, it also predicted His resurrection in Psalm 16:8–11 and refers to His eternal reign. The only way to reconcile these verses is that Jesus is the Messiah who died then rose again.

---

[29] Peter Carsten Theide and Matthew D'Ancona, *Eyewitness to Jesus* (New York: Doubleday, 1996), p. 163.

Jesus Himself made these predictions in regard to His resurrection: "Destroy this temple and in three days, I will raise it up." (John 2:19). In Mark 8:31 Jesus taught "that the son of Man must suffer many things . . . and be killed, and after three days rise again." In John 10:18 Jesus stated, "I have authority to lay it (My life) down, and I have authority to take it up again." In these passages, Jesus predicted His own death and resurrection. Either Jesus was mad, or He really had authority over death.

Jesus' resurrection proved His authority over sin and death. At the beginning of this study we examined the claims of Christ. We realized only three conclusions were possible: liar, lunatic, or Lord. Since the first two were inconceivable, we needed to see if Christ could further confirm His credentials of being God. We discovered that the record of prophecy, His miracles, and the Resurrection confirmed His claims.

Nineteen centuries have come and gone, and today He is the central figure for much of the human race. All the armies that ever marched, and all the navies that ever sailed, and all the parliaments that ever sat, and all the kings that ever reigned, put together have not affected the life of man upon this earth as powerfully as this *One Solitary Life.*[30]

---

[30] Anonymous, "One Solitary Life," quoted in Tim LaHaye, *Jesus, Who Is He?*, p. 8

Chapter 6
See the Risen Lord

Throughout the centuries, there have been scholars who have attempted to deny the account of the Resurrection. Our schools are filled with history books that give alternative explanations for the Resurrection or in some cases, fail to even mention this unique event. In this chapter, we will look at the evidence supporting the Resurrection to determine if this event is historical fact or fiction.

Science and History

I am often challenged by skeptics to prove the Resurrection scientifically. However, the scientific method cannot be applied to the Resurrection or any historical event for that matter. The scientific method determines "fact" based on experimentation and repeated observations. We begin with a hypothesis, which is tested repeatedly and observed. When the data and results confirm the hypothesis, we acknowledge it as a verified theory. Therefore, this method is limited to *repeatable* events or observable objects. Historical events cannot be repeated. Therefore, we cannot apply the scientific method to verify historical occurrences.

I have described the scientific method and then asked the skeptic, "Using that method, prove the life events of Julius Caesar." I have had men and women draw diagrams of equations, charts, and other figures in an attempt to meet the criteria. In the end, it was clear the life events of Julius Caesar could not be proven through repeatable observation. Then I stated, "Since Julius Caesar is not proven by the scientific method, we must conclude that we cannot know anything about Julius Caesar, not even his very existence." Of course no one ever accepted that proposition. It is at this point most realized that in proving historical facts, we must use the historical method of proof not the scientific method.

In the historical method, a historian gathers evidence, oral accounts, written accounts, and artifacts. Upon further study, he reconstructs a picture of the past. He attempts to provide the most reasonable and plausible explanation for the evidence at hand. An event can be considered historical knowledge when we can demonstrate the conclusion is reasonable and consistent with the evidence.

A jury is asked to make a decision based, not on mathematical certainty, but beyond reasonable doubt. In the same way when it comes to the historical method, the issue is the greatest probability not mathematical certainty.

To prove a historical event like the Resurrection, we must look at the historical evidence. Thus far we have shown that belief in the historical Jesus of the New Testament has been verified. Now we will examine the historical facts concerning the Resurrection to see what the evidence reveals.

Examining the Evidence

Five major and undisputed facts must be reckoned with when investigating the Resurrection: the empty tomb, the transformation of the Apostles, the preaching of the Resurrection originating in Jerusalem, a massive Jewish societal transformation, and the origin of the church.

The Empty Tomb

Let us first examine the evidence of the empty tomb. Jesus was a well-known figure in Israel. Many people knew His burial site. In fact, Matthew recorded the exact location of Jesus' tomb. He stated, "And Joseph of Arimathea took the body and wrapped it in a clean linen cloth and laid it in his own new tomb." (Matthew 27:59) Mark asserted that Joseph was "a prominent member of the Council." (Mark 15:43) It would have been destructive for the writers to invent a man of such prominence, name him specifically, and designate the tomb site, since eyewitnesses could have easily discredited the author's fallacious claims.

Jewish and Roman sources both testified to an empty tomb. Matthew 28:12–13 specifically states that the chief priests invented the story that the disciples stole the body. There would be no need for this fabrication if the tomb had not truly been empty. Opponents of the Resurrection had to account for the empty tomb. If the tomb had not been empty, the preaching of the Apostles could not have continued. All the Jewish authorities needed to do to put an end to Christianity was to produce the body of Jesus. Along with the empty tomb is the fact that the corpse of Jesus was never found. Not one historical record from the first or second century is written attacking the factuality of the empty tomb or claiming discovery of the corpse. Tom Anderson, former president of the California Trial Lawyers Association, stated,

> Let's assume that the written accounts of His appearances to hundreds of people are false. I want to pose a question.

With an event so well publicized, don't you think that it's reasonable that one historian, one eyewitness, one antagonist would record for all time that he had seen Christ's body? . . . The silence of history is deafening when it comes to the testimony against the resurrection.[31]

The Transformed Lives of the Apostles

Second, we have the changed lives of the Apostles. It is recorded in the gospels that while Jesus was on trial, the Apostles deserted Him in fear of the Jewish authorities. However, just a few days later, they were transformed to bold preachers of the resurrected Christ, preaching the message in the midst of hostile surroundings. All eleven abandoned their occupations, put their lives and the lives of their families at risk, and even traveled to distant countries to proclaim the good news. What best accounts for this transformation? It must have been a very compelling event.

The Preaching of the Resurrection Originated in Jerusalem

Third, the Apostles began preaching the Resurrection in Jerusalem. This is significant since this was the very city in which Jesus was crucified. It was still extremely hostile. Furthermore, all the evidence was there for everyone to investigate. Legends take root in foreign lands or centuries after the event. Discrediting such legends is difficult since the facts are hard to verify. However, in this case the preaching occured in the city of the event immediately after it happened. The enemies of Christ were seeking any way they could to discredit the testimony of the Apostles. Every possible fact could have been and probably was investigated thoroughly.

---

[31] Josh McDowell, *The Resurrection Factor* (San Bernadino, Calif.: Here's Life Publishers, 1981), p. 66.

Massive Jewish Societal Transformation

Fourth, we had a massive Jewish societal transformation. For the Jews, the Law of Moses had been taught for 1500 years. This sacred law distinguished them as God's people. What best accounts for thousands of Jews immediately abandoning major practices of the Jewish law?

Shortly after the preaching of the Apostles, thousands of Jews abandoned the sacrificial ceremony at the Temple of Jerusalem where the most sacred of ceremonies were conducted for the nation. They also began worshipping on a Sunday rather than observing the traditional Sabbath day, Saturday. This strictly monotheistic society adopted the doctrine of a triune God, one God revealed in three persons, the Father, the Son and the Holy Spirit. The Jewish nation believed obedience to the Law of Moses was essential for salvation. What best accounts for this sudden transformation?

The Origin of the Church

Finally, we have the origin of the church which built their foundation on the preaching of a resurrected Messiah. It is very unlikely that the church could have thrived as it did, amongst a governing council that sought to discredit its testimony in any way, unless their central proclamation was true. Anyone questioning the Resurrection must somehow explain these five facts.

Attempted Explanations

Over the years, five arguments have been used to disprove the Resurrection. They are: the wrong tomb theory, the hallucination theory, the swoon theory, the stolen body theory, the sleeping soldiers theory, and most recently the theory that wild dogs ate the body of Jesus.

The Wrong Tomb Theory

Kirsop Lake introduced this argument in 1907. According to the gospels, the women visited the grave early in the morning while it was dark. Due to their emotional condition and the darkness, they visited the wrong tomb. Overjoyed to see that it was empty, they rushed back to tell the disciples Jesus had risen. The disciples, in turn, ran into Jerusalem to proclaim the Resurrection.

There are several major flaws with this explanation. First, it is extremely doubtful that the Apostles would not have corrected the women's error. The Gospel of John gives a very detailed account of them doing just that. Second, the tomb site was known not only by the followers of Christ but also by their opponents. If the body still remained in the tomb as the Apostles began preaching, the authorities simply would go to the right tomb, produce the body, and march it down the streets. This would have ended the Christian faith once and for all. Remember that the preaching of the Resurrection began in Jerusalem, minutes away from the site of the crucifixion and tomb. These factors make the theory of a wrong tomb extremely weak.

The Hallucination Theory

The second theory introduced by David Friedrich Straus in 1835, holds that the Resurrection of Christ just occurred in the minds of the disciples. Other historians have since built onto his argument. Dr. William McNeil articulated this position in his book, *A World History*. He wrote,

> The Roman authorities in Jerusalem arrested and
> crucified Jesus. . . . But soon afterwards the dispirited
> Apostles gathered in an upstairs room and suddenly felt
> again the heartwarming presence of their master. This
> seemed absolutely convincing evidence that Jesus' death
> on the cross had not been the end but the beginning. . .
> The Apostles bubbled over with excitement and tried to
> explain to all who would listen all that had happened.[32]

This position is unrealistic for several reasons. In order for
hallucinations of this type to occur, psychiatrists agree that several
conditions must exist. First, hallucinations generally occur to
people who are imaginative and of a nervous makeup. However,
the appearances of Jesus occurred to a variety of people. Second,
hallucinations are subjective and individual. No two people have
the same experience. Yet in this case, over five hundred people (1
Corinthians 15) had the same account. Third, hallucinations
occur only at particular times and places and are associated with
the events. The Resurrection appearances occured in many different environments and at different times. Finally, hallucinations of this nature occur to those who intensely want to believe.
However, several witnesses such as Thomas and James, the half
brother of Jesus, were initially hostile to the news of the
Resurrection.

If some continue to argue for this position, they still must
account for the empty tomb. If the Apostles dreamed up the
Resurrection during their preaching, all the authorities needed to
do was produce the body and that would have ended the
Apostles' dream.

---

[32] William McNeil, *A World History* (New York: Oxford University Press, 1979), p. 163.

The Swoon Theory

A third theory espouses that Jesus never died on the cross but merely passed out and was mistakenly considered dead. After three days He revived, exited the tomb, and appeared to His disciples who believed He had risen from the dead. This theory was developed in the early nineteenth century by Friedrich Schleirmaker, but today it has been completely discounted for several reasons.

First, it is a physical impossibility that Jesus could have survived the tortures of the crucifixion. Second, the soldiers who crucified Jesus were experts in executing this type of death penalty. Furthermore, they took several precautions to make sure He was actually dead. They thrust a spear in His side. When blood and water come out separately, the blood cells have begun to separate from the plasma which will only happen when the blood stops circulating. Upon determining to break the legs of the criminals (in order to speed up the process of dying), the guards carefully examined the body of Jesus and found that He was already dead.

After being taken down from the cross, Jesus' body was covered with eighty pounds of spices and embalmed. It is unreasonable to believe that after three days with no food or water, Jesus would revive. Even harder to believe is that Jesus could roll a two-ton stone that blocked the entrance up an incline to open the tomb, overpower the guards posted there, and then walk several miles to Emmaeus. Even if Jesus had managed this feat, His appearing to the disciples half-dead and desperately in need of medical attention would not have prompted their worship of Him as God.

Even David F. Strauss who proposed the hallucination theory, put an end to any hope in the swoon theory. Although he did not believe in the Resurrection, he concluded:

It is impossible that a being who had stolen half-dead out of the sepulchre, who crept about weak and ill, wanting medical treatment, who required bandaging, strengthening, and indulgence, and who still at last yielded to his sufferings, could have given the disciples the impression that he was a Conqueror over death and the grave, the Prince of life, an impression that would lay at the bottom of their future ministry.[33]

The Stolen Body Theory

This fourth argument holds that Jewish and Roman authorities stole the body or moved it for safekeeping. It is inconceivable to think this a possibility. If they had the body, why did they need to accuse the disciples of stealing it? (Matthew 28:11–15) In Acts 4, the Jewish authorities were angry and did everything they could to prevent the spread of Christianity. Why would the authorities deceive their own people into believing in a false Messiah when they knew that this deception would mean the deaths of hundreds of their believing friends? If they really knew where the body was, they could have exposed it and ended the faith that caused them so much trouble and embarrassment. Throughout the preaching of the Apostles, the authorities never attempted to refute the Resurrection by producing a body. This theory has little merit.

The Sleeping Soldiers Theory

The fifth and most popular theory has existed since the day of the Resurrection and is still believed by many opponents of Christianity. Matthew 28:12–13 articulates this position.

---

[33] David Strauss, *The Life of Jesus for the People*, vol. 1, 2nd edition (London: Williams and Norgate, 1879), p. 412.

When the chief priests had met with the elders and devised a plan, they gave the soldiers a large sum of money telling them, "You are to say, his disciples came during the night and stole him away while we were asleep."

Many have wondered why Matthew recorded this and then did not refute it. Perhaps it is because this explanation was so preposterous, he did not see the need to do so.

This explanation remains an impossibility for several reasons. First, if the soldiers were sleeping, how did they know it was the disciples who stole the body? Second, it seems physically impossible for the disciples to sneak past the soldiers and then move a two-ton stone up an incline in absolute silence. Certainly the guards would have heard something.

Third, the tomb was secured with a Roman seal. Anyone who moved the stone would have to break the seal, an offense punishable by death. The depression and cowardice of the disciples makes it difficult to believe that they would suddenly become so brave as to face a detachment of soldiers, steal the body, and then lie about the Resurrection when they would ultimately face a life of suffering and death for their contrived message.

Fourth, Roman guards were not likely to fall asleep with such an important duty. There were penalties for doing so. Further, the disciples would have needed to overpower them, a very unlikely scenario. Finally, in the Gospel of John, the grave clothes were found "lying there as well as the burial cloth that had been around Jesus' head. The cloth was folded up by itself separate from the linen." (John 20:6-7) There was not enough time for the disciples to sneak past the guards, roll away the stone, unwrap the body, rewrap it in their wrappings, and fold the headpiece neatly next to the linen. In a robbery, the men would have flung the garments down in disarray and fled for fear of detection.

Wild Dogs Ate the Body

A recent explanation has been introduced by one of the leaders of the Jesus Seminar, John Dominic Crossan. He argues that the body of Jesus was thrown in a shallow grave and eaten by wild dogs. He wrote,

> If the Romans did not observe the Deuteronomic decree, Jesus' dead body would have been left on the cross for wild beasts. And his followers, who had fled would know that. If the Romans did observe the decree, the soldiers would have made certain Jesus was dead and then buried him themselves as part of their job. In either case his body left on the cross or in a shallow grave barely covered with dirt and stones, the dogs were waiting. And his followers who had fled, would know that too.[34]

I respect Crossan's credentials as I do the other scholars mentioned, but his theory does not honestly deal with the facts related to the crucifixion account given in the gospels. First, this theory was not suggested until nearly two thousand years after the fact. It seems strange that the opponents of Christianity failed to mention this as an explanation. Instead they offered an explanation that the disciples stole the body while the guards slept. This alternative would not be necessary if people knew the fate of Jesus' body. Finally, the gospels go to great lengths to identify the tomb. They name the owner, Joseph of Arimathea, a member of the ruling council. But Crossan argues that this is a fictitious character. He stated,

---

[34] John Dominic Crossan, *Jesus, A Revolutionary Biography*, (san Francisco: Harper Collins Publisher, 1989), p. 154.

The dilemma is painfully clear. Political authority had crucified Jesus and was against him. But, his followers knew, it also took authority or at least authority's permission to bury him. How could one have it both ways? ... Mark 15:42–46 solves the problem by creating one Joseph of Arimathea.[35]

As indicated earlier, it would have been disastrous for the gospel writers to make up a character and give him such a high profile position in society. This fact could have easily been discredited by the eyewitnesses. Imagine if I invented a judge on the Supreme Court of the United States and stated he made a major ruling that affected key institutions of our country. I could easily be discredited. The same is true here. If the disciples invented Joseph, their testimony would have easily been proven false. If they went on to invent the account of the Roman guards at the tomb, they would only compound their problems.

Crossan's argument is not consistent with the facts that surround the crucifixion of Christ. It is clear the tomb site was known, secured, and empty on the third day.

Conclusion: Monumental Implications

These theories inadequately account for the empty tomb, the transformation of the Apostles, and the birth of Christianity in the city of the crucifixion. The conclusion we must seriously consider is that Jesus rose from the grave. The implications are monumental.

First, if Jesus rose from the dead, then what He said about Himself is true. He stated, "I am the Resurrection and the life; he who believes in Me shall live even if he dies." (John 11:25) He also stated, "I am the way, and the truth, and the life; no man comes

---

[35] Ibid., 156.

to the Father, but through Me." (John 14:6) Eternal life is found through Jesus Christ alone. Any religious belief that contradicts this must be false. Other religious leaders are buried in graves and their tombs have become places of worship. The location of Jesus' tomb is unknown because it is empty; His body is not there. There was no need to enshrine an empty tomb. The Resurrection sets Christianity apart from all other religions.

Second, Paul wrote in 1 Corinthians 15:54, "Death has been swallowed up in victory." Physical death is not the end. Eternal life with our Lord awaits all who trust in Him because Jesus has conquered death.

Chapter 7
See the Only Way

Don't All Religions Lead to God?

*I*s there only one way to eternal salvation or are there numerous paths one can follow? On this crucial issue there are three primary views: pluralism, inclusivism, and exclusivism.

Religious pluralism views all religions as equally valid. This view is illustrated in an eastern pantheist story. Four blind men come upon an elephant. One grabs the trunk, one the tail, one the ear, and the last the foot. The four men describe the same animal in different and contradictory ways. One says an elephant is a vertical snake-like object. Another says it is short and skinny with hair on the end. Another describes the elephant as flat and wide. Yet another describes it as being round and heavy like a tree stump. All four men are describing the same object but their contradicting conclusions are the result of their blindness. They cannot see the total picture.

That is an illustration of the differing world religions. Pluralists believe all religions are describing the same God and in essence the same beliefs. Since we are all blind and do not have the total picture, we each describe God and salvation in different and seemingly opposing ways. However if we could just see the total picture, we would realize we are all essentially united and heading for the same eternal destination.

Inclusivism is the view that although Jesus is the exclusive savior, many, who have never explicitly trusted nor heard of Jesus, will be saved. God accepts those with implicit or sincere faith. This faith may come in response to the general revelation of creation and the conscience or through truths in other religions.

Exclusivism is the belief that Jesus is the only savior and explicit faith in Him alone is necessary for salvation.

In our present day, pluralism is the most widely accepted view. Among Christians, exclusivism has been the historic view. However, a growing number of denominations have adopted the views of inclusivism and even pluralism. Christian exclusivism has been labeled intolerant, prejudiced, or narrow-minded. But the Bible supports a Christian exclusivist view.

Evidence from the teachings of Jesus and the Apostles point to exclusivism. In John 14:6 Jesus stated, "I am the way, the truth and the life. No one comes to the Father except through Me." Jesus did not say, "I am a way" but "*the* way." He reinforces this with the phrase: "No one comes to the Father *except through Me.*" Access to the Father can only come through Jesus.

The Apostles repeated His claim of exclusivity. In Acts 4:12 Peter stated, "Salvation is found in no one else, for there is no other name under heaven given to men by which we must be saved." Paul states in 1 Timothy 2:5, "For there is one God and one mediator between God and men, the man Christ Jesus." From these passages and others the Apostles clearly state that Jesus is the only way to eternal salvation.

Another evidence to support exclusivism is the missionary zeal of the early church. The Apostles and new Christians traveled to all reaches of the Roman Empire sacrificing their families and their lives to share the good news of Jesus. What accounts for the missionary zeal and urgency if there are alternate ways to eternal life? It would not have been necessary to preach

Jesus since those who have never heard had alternate ways to heaven. The obvious answer is salvation is found in no one else but Jesus.

Aren't All Religions the Same?

Many believe that all religions are essentially the same and therefore, it really doesn't matter what you believe as long as you are sincere about your religion. One argument is that within all religions there are many similarities. Don't these similarities prove that all religions are in essence the same?

Although there are some similarities between all religions, we must be aware that similarity does not imply sameness. A comparative study of the religions quickly reveals that they are vastly different in their fundamental beliefs. They contradict one another on key issues such as the nature of the divine, salvation, sin, and the nature of man.

Let us begin with the concept of the divine. There are many sects in Hinduism that teach various views. The most popular concept of God in Hinduism is that the divine or Brahma is an impersonal force or energy that is made up of all things in the universe. The universe contains God and the universe is God. This view is called Pantheism. Buddha says very little about God in his teachings. God does not play a major role in one attaining salvation. Several schools of Buddhism are atheistic. Centuries after Buddha's death some sects deified him and hold to a belief that over the centuries, there have been many incarnations of Buddha. In Islam, Allah, as described in the Koran, is impersonal and mainly seen as a God of judgment and wrath. He is responsible for good as well as evil acts. Christianity teaches there is one God who is revealed in three persons, the Father, the Son and the Holy Spirit, the Trinity. God is an all-powerful and loving being who is not a part of creation but rules over the universe as the sustainer and creator of all. God loves man so much, He gave His only Son to reveal Himself to us and sacrificed His life to rescue us from eternal death.

All religions differ in their teaching on the nature of man. In Hinduism, man is divine but trapped in the physical body. In Buddhism, man is entrapped in this world of suffering due to his desires. Muslims believe man is not sinful in nature but weak and in need of guidance. In the Bible, all men from Adam are born with a sin nature and alienated from God.

All religions differ greatly in their salvation message. Non-Christian religions teach that one must earn his salvation through good works. Whether it is following the path of devotion, or path of works, or path of knowledge in Hinduism, or the eightfold path of Buddhism, or the five pillars of Islam, one must work for it. The Bible states in Ephesians 2:8–9 "For it is by grace you have been saved through faith and this not from yourselves It is a gift from God, not by works so that no one can boast." In Christianity, salvation is a free gift, to be received because of the finished work of Christ on the cross. Christianity teaches that God reached down to help us but in other religions, humans are working to reach up to God. Since Christianity teaches salvation is based on God's finished work on the cross, it alone offers assurance of salvation.

The religions differ in their concept of sin, an offense against God's moral law. In Hinduism and Buddhism, an individual soul does not exist, it is an illusion to the unenlightened. Therefore, they do not recognize sin and moral guilt against a moral divine being. Man's root problem is ignorance of truth. In Islam, there exists no original sin. Humans are basically good, but fallible and need guidance. Sin is the rejection of right guidance and can be forgiven by repentance. No atonement is necessary.

After the resurrection, each man's deeds will be weighed to determine his fate. Christianity teaches that sin separates men from God. It is the cause of spiritual death. (Romans 6:23) Forgiveness comes only by the sacrifice of Jesus.

The destiny of man is contradictory as well. In Hinduism and Buddhism, man is in an endless cycle of reincarnation. His form in the next rebirth is determined by the quality of moral life one has lived. This cycle continues until it is broken and one reaches Nirvana. In Hinduism, Nirvana is reuniting with Brahma. One's individuality ceases and is absorbed into the divine, like a drop of water returning to the ocean. In Buddhism, Nirvana is a state of total nothingness. Here all consciousness ceases. It is a state of emptiness. In Islam, each man's deeds is weighed to determine his fate in heaven or hell. Islamic paradise consists of enjoying wine, song, and the entertainment of heavenly maidens. In Christianity, all men and women will stand before the judgment seat of Christ. At this time the eternal fate of each individual will be determined once and for all. There is no second chance or reincarnation cycle. (Hebrews 9:27) Believers go to heaven with Jesus while unbelievers suffer eternal punishment in hell.

Of all the great religious leaders, Christ alone claimed to be God. Buddha claimed to be the "Way Shower". Muhammad claimed to be the prophet of Allah. None claimed to be divine accept Jesus. Other religions reject this idea that Jesus is God incarnate. All of Christianity centers on the person of Jesus Christ. In all other religions, one can remove the founder and still maintain the faith. One can remove Buddha and still have Buddhism. One can remove Muhammad and still have Islam. These men emphasized their teachings. Christianity centers on the person of Christ. He is the way, He is the life, and He is the ultimate revelation of truth.

From just a brief overview of the basic fundamentals of each religion, we see that they differ in significant ways. We cannot say all religions are in essence the same, nor can we say they are all right at the same time. According to Aristotle's law of non-contradiction, two opposites cannot be true in a relationship with one another at the same time. Their beliefs on fundamental tenets appear to be mutually incompatible. Is God an impersonal force made up of the universe or is He a personal being who is separate from and rules over creation? Is man divine in nature, essentially good, or corrupted by sin and separated from God? Is salvation a matter of attaining enlightenment, of doing good works, or not attainable in any way by man, but must be received as a gift from God? At death, does one enter an endless cycle of reincarnation, or does one stand in a final judgement before God, sentenced to eternal life or eternal punishment? We cannot say all these opposing doctrines are true at the same time without radically altering our definition of truth.

What Are His Credentials?

Jesus made it clear, that He is the only way to eternal life (John 14:6), upholding the doctrine called Christian exclusivity. After making such claims, how do we know Jesus had the authority to make such claims, and did He demonstrate them to be true? We know that the Bible is a historically accurate document. (See chapter 3) Thus, according to the Bible, Jesus demonstrated the right and authority as God to set the criteria for salvation.

As we discussed earlier, Jesus demonstrated supremacy over all creation, authorities, principalities, and powers. In the Gospel accounts, He exhibited authority over creation by calming the storm, turning water into wine, and multiplying food. He displayed command over sickness by curing those inflicted with terminal diseases and physical ailments. He exhibited power over the spiritual realm by casting out demons. He demonstrated dominion over time. The prophecies he fulfilled show a clear control over history. No leader has ever demonstrated authority over all these elements.

The ultimate proof lies in his power over sin and death. All religious leaders struggled with the cleansing of sin and have yielded to death. Only Jesus conquered sin and death. He showed mastery over sin by living a sinless life. In John 8 Jesus challenged His opposition by asking them this question, "Can any of you prove me guilty of sin?" To this challenge, His enemies could not name a single sin. Their only accusation was that His power and works came from another source other than God.

In Mark 2, Jesus demonstrated His authority to forgive sins. Upon seeing a paralytic man on a stretcher, He declared the man forgiven of all sin. To further prove His spiritual claims, He healed the man physically to validate the authority of His claims.

Finally Jesus confirmed His rule over the ultimate enemy, death. On several occasions Jesus raised the dead. (John 11 and Mark 5) Most convincing is the fact that Jesus raised Himself from the dead. The Resurrection of Christ is the ultimate proof of His supremacy over sin and death.

Romans 6:23 states that sin separates us from a holy God and the result of sin is death or eternal separation from Him. Sin and death are the unvanquished foes. However in Christ, these foes are defeated at the cross. Colossians 2:15 states, "And having disarmed the powers and authorities, He made a public spectacle of them, triumphing over them by the cross." All other great religious leaders are in the grave. Jesus is alive!

Jesus is the only way, for He demonstrated the authority over all creation and the forces that keep us separated from God. The way to eternal life is found in the one who has the authority to grant it: Jesus Christ.

What about Those Who Never Heard?

We established the argument that Jesus is the only way to eternal life with God. The resulting question asked is what about those who have never had a chance to hear the Gospel? Is God righteous in judging them?

Paul addresses this question in the first two chapters of Romans. Romans 1:18-20 states,

> The wrath of God is being revealed from heaven against all the godlessness and wickedness of men who suppress the truth by their wickedness, since what may be known about God is plain to them, because God has made it plain to them. For since the creation of the world God's invisible qualities—His eternal power and divine nature—have been clearly seen, being understood from what has been made, so that men are without excuse.

Besides the special revelation of the Bible and Jesus Christ, God has revealed Himself to all mankind through the witness of natural revelation or creation and the conscience. Chapter 1 proclaims that everything that exists in the universe testifies to the invisible qualities and divine nature of God. When one investigates creation, one must conclude a divine intelligence exists.

As a famous physicist stated, "All that I have seen gives me faith in the creator for all that I have not seen." For this reason, Paul stated the witness of creation is made plain to all men and all men are "without excuse."

The second revelation of God is the witness of the conscience. Romans 2:14-16 states,

Indeed, when the gentiles who do not have the law, do by nature things required by the law, they are a law for themselves, even though they do not have the law, since they show that the requirements of the law are written on their hearts, their consciences also bearing witness, and their thoughts now accusing, now even defending them.

The conscience functions as an implanted code of law in people. The virtues of love, justice, wisdom, and courage pervade in every culture. Not only does our conscience reveal right and wrong, it also testifies that a divine lawgiver exists. From this passage we conclude, all humankind have an intuitive knowledge that a God exists and He has given mankind a moral law.

The Witness of General Revelation Confirmed by Anthropology

Anthropologists have also confirmed this principle. Due to the influence of Darwinian evolutionary thought, many anthropologists taught that the oldest religion in the world was animism which later evolved into monotheism. However, anthropologists studying the origin of religions have made a strong case revealing that the first form of religion is monotheism which was later abandoned and replaced by polytheism.

Anthropologist Wilhelm Schmidt wrote a 4,000-page treatise, *The Origin and Growth of Religion*, documenting this. Don Richardson has recently confirmed this conclusion as well in his book, *Eternity in Their Hearts*. In the numerous cultures Schmidt and Richardson studied throughout the world from primitive to highly developed religions, societies began with an original belief built on the concept of a God who is the creator of all and who is a moral law giver. He receives the worship of the people. Eventually, the people turn away from Him and begin to worship other deities.

The *Encyclopedia of Religion and Ethics* states that the Chinese culture before Confucianism, Buddhism and Taoism, 2600 years before Christ, worshipped Shang Ti. They understood Him to be the creator and law-giver. They believed that He was never to be represented by an idol. When the Zhou Dynasty took control of China in 1066–770 B.C., the worship of Shang Ti was replaced by the worship of heaven itself and eventually the other three religions entered China. In the Korean culture, it was discovered they worshipped a similar God called Hananim who was the creator and law-giver.

In a region north of Calcutta, India, there lived the Santal people. They were found worshipping elements of nature. However, before these practices developed, they worshipped Thakur Jiu, the Genuine God who created all things. Although they knew Thakur Jiu was the true God, the tribe forsook worshipping Him and began entering into spiritism and worship of lesser gods who ruled over some aspect of creation. In Ethiopia, the Gedeo numbered in the millions and lived in different tribes. These people sacrificed to evil spirits out of fear. However, behind this practice was an older belief in Magano, the one omnipotent creator. In the Central African Republic there were the Mbaka tribesmen whom Baptist missionaries discovered in the early 1920's. These people held to a belief in Koro, the creator. This tribe worshipped Koro but eventually turned away from Him and lost the truth they knew of Koro. The Inca's in South America also have this same belief. Alfred Metraux, author of *History of the Incas*, discovered the Incas originally worshipped Viracocha, the Lord, the omnipotent creator of all things. Worship of Inti, the Sun God, and other gods are only recent departures from this monotheistic belief.[36]

This is consistent with the book of Genesis and the Romans 1 passage. Man originally worshipped the God of the

---

[36] Don Richardson, *Eternity in Their Hearts* (Ventura: CA.: Regal Books, 1984) pp. 33-71.

Bible and after turning away from Him at the Tower of Babel
(Genesis 11), they fell into idolatry.

Romans 1:21 summarizes this progression.

For although they knew God, they neither glorified
Him as God nor gave thanks to Him, but in their foolish
hearts were darkened. Although they claimed to be wise,
they became fools and exchanged the glory of the
immortal God for images made to look like mortal man
and birds and animals and reptiles.

Schmidt, Richardson and other anthropologists docu-
mented numerous cultures supporting the fact that monotheism
is the oldest form of religion and the original God worshipped
matches the character described in the Bible. We can conclude
that what Paul wrote in Romans is true, all men have the witness
of God through creation and his moral law is embedded into
their conscience.

From General Revelation to Special Revelation

Scripture states when an individual acknowledges natural
revelation, then God is responsible to bring special revelation to
that individual. If one rejects the witness of natural revelation,
God is not obligated to bring the message to him. Even so, God
often does bring the message because of His mercy and grace.

An example from Scripture is that of Cornelius in Acts,
Chapter 10. Cornelius was a Roman soldier who feared God but
did not have knowledge of Jesus. Since he acknowledged the witness of natural revelation, God sent Peter to bring the good news.

Don Richardson tells of modern-day examples of this principle in his book, *Eternity in Their Hearts*. Richardson recorded numerous accounts of missionaries who traveled to distant lands where the Gospel had never been preached and discovered the people there were waiting to hear the message of Jesus Christ.

One story is recorded of a tribe in Burma called the Karen. From what they saw of creation and what they knew in their hearts, they acknowledged a divine being. During their late night teaching sessions, they went out into the jungle and prayed that the God who created all things would make Himself known to them. They knew their prayers were answered when two Christian missionaries appeared and shared the Gospel message with them.[37]

God is just in judging all men for we all have the witness of creation and the conscience. When one acknowledges these witnesses, God will bring the Gospel message, because it is His desire that no one should perish but all come to saving knowledge of His love and forgiveness.

---

[37] Ibid., 73-85.

Chapter 8
See the Answer to Evil

*J*n the previous chapters I have been making a case for the Christian faith. In this chapter we face the toughest question a Christian must answer. If God exists, what accounts for all the evil in the world? If we have a God who is good, loving, and sovereign, how do we account for evil which is contrary to His nature? In dealing with this challenge, we must address two aspects of the issue, the philosophical problem of evil and the personal problem of evil. The philosophical aspect addresses the question, "Does the existence of evil argue against the existence of God?" The personal aspect deals with the struggles that come when an individual experiences evil and suffering.

The Philosophical Problem of Evil

Let us begin by affirming the character of God as revealed in the Bible. God is morally good; He is just, loving, and sovereign over all creation. Evil is contrary to the nature of God, in fact, He hates it. The paradigm used to argue against the existence of God looks like this:

An all powerful God could destroy evil.
An all loving God would destroy evil.

Evil is not destroyed.
Therefore an all loving and powerful God does not exist.

The Origin of Evil

If God were as caring and omnipotent as the Bible says, then why is there still pain in the world? In order to get a satisfactory answer, we must understand the origin of evil. God, in His great love, created man in His image. This means He created man to reflect some of the moral attributes of God. Part of being made in the image of God means man has the capacity to love and has a free will. Free will allows man to be the only creature that can have a love relationship with God.

It is impossible for love to exist without free will. Love is not love if it is forced upon someone. In a relationship of love, the other being must exercise free will and choose to enter into the relationship. In love God created man with the capacity to exercise his free will and choose to obey or disobey Him. With freedom there exists the capacity for evil.

For example, let's say I give one of my students the keys to my car and ask, "Could you go and pick up a pizza?" Giving him this freedom is not evil. However, he can use his freedom for evil. He can obey my wishes, or he can choose to go drag racing on the interstate freeway. Freedom creates the potential for evil. Adam in his freedom, chose to disobey God and thus sin entered into the world. That event was the origin of evil.

Why Does God Allow Evil to Exist?

The next question is, why does God allow evil and does that negate His sovereignty? Just because God allows evil to exist does not mean He is not in control. God is allowing evil to persist and, in His sovereignty, is using evil to accomplish His purpose. Often in the Bible, what appeared to be the triumph of evil, turned out to be the triumph of God's ultimate plan.

In Genesis 37 Joseph was betrayed by his brothers and sold into slavery in Egypt. Despite this evil act, God used it to bring about His purpose in shaping the character of Joseph, to be a future ruler who would preserve the nation of Israel during a famine. In the end, Joseph saw how God used this apparent tragedy to bring about His purpose. He stated in Genesis 50:19–21 to his brothers, "Am I in the place of God? You intended to harm me, but God intended it for good to accomplish what is now being done, the saving of many lives." God overcame evil and accomplished His purpose.

The cross is the greatest illustration of good coming from evil. It appeared that evil had triumphed, as a friend of the Lord Jesus betrayed Him, the religious rulers falsely accused Him, and the soldiers beat Him for hours. After suffering the cruel torture of crucifixion, Jesus tasted the ultimate death, separation from His Father. Yet this tragic event fell right into the plan of God to bring salvation to men who trust Jesus as Lord and Savior. So God maintains His sovereignty in allowing evil to exist to fulfill His purpose.

Will God always allow evil to exist? No. God will allow evil to exist until He has fulfilled His purpose, and then He will destroy evil. Why? Because of His grace. 2 Peter 3:9 states, "The Lord is not slow in keeping His promise, as some understand slowness. He is patient with you, not wanting anyone to perish, but everyone to come to repentance." In other words, God withholds the destruction of evil so that more who are opposed to God can turn and receive His grace. I am glad God did not destroy evil in 1980. If He did, I would be in hell, eternally separated from Him today. God's grace and mercy will not extend indefinitely.

One day He will execute His justice and bring evil to an end.

A New Paradigm

The argument against God from the existence of evil makes a false presumption. Just because evil is not yet defeated, does not mean it will always remain this way. Though God has not removed evil today, it does not mean that He never will. If we take into account that the final chapter of God's dealing with mankind is not finished, the new paradigm is the following:

> God is all-powerful and can defeat evil.
> God is loving and will defeat evil.
> Evil is not yet defeated.
> God can and will defeat evil at a future time.

The existence of evil does not argue against the existence of God. God is using evil to accomplish His purpose as He waits patiently for more to receive His gift of grace. We must also wait and trust Him to bring all things to His final conclusion.

The Personal Problem of Evil

The philosophical problem of evil answers the intellectual challenge. For those who have experienced the cruelty of evil, we offer answers that can bring healing, peace, and strength. Only God's Word can provide hope. There are no easy solutions nor quick fixes that will instantly remove the pain one feels in such times. Even the great Christians suffered and wrestled with the issue. Yet of all the world views, I believe the Christian world view offers the explanations that are true and the most meaningful.

How does the Christian face the pain of suffering that comes from experiencing evil? First, understand we live in a fallen world that is suffering the consequences of sin. Mankind in his free will has chosen to turn away and seeks to live life with no regard for God or His laws. In His grace, God does not impose His will on man and has allowed mankind to temporarily go his or her own way. The apostle John wrote in 1 John 2:15-16,

> Do not love the world or anything in the world. If any one loves the world, the love of the Father is not in Him. For everything in the world—the cravings of sinful man, the lust of the eyes and the boasting of what he has and does—comes not from the Father but from the world.

John was not stating here that we are not to love the people in the world. He was saying the system of the world is in rebellion to God. Therefore, we suffer the results. Because we live in this world we are not immune to its effects.

Second, the verse from John goes on to state, "The world and its desires pass away, but the man who does the will of God lives forever." (1 John 2:17) Although we live in a fallen world and suffer the effects of evil, it will not always be this way. One day, God will bring an end to all evil and suffering. The pain we suffer now reminds us of our need to depend on God and not ourselves for ultimate hope and to desire the day when He will restore all things. Paul wrote in 2 Corinthians 4:17, "For momentary, light affliction is producing for us an eternal weight of glory far beyond comparison." Promises like these bring us hope even in the face of hopeless situations.

Third, we draw comfort from knowing God understands our suffering and cares for our situation. God understands because

He endured the greatest pain on the cross. He cares deeply about us especially in our moments of suffering. 1 Peter 5:7 states, "Cast all your anxiety on Him because He cares for you." God never abandons His people and wants us to draw near to Him in our time of need.

Fourth, God remains in control of all things and He is at work in every situation. He has a purpose for our life that is always for His glory and our good. Romans 8:28 states, "And we know that in all things God works for the good of those who love Him, who have been called according to His purpose." No matter how bad the situation may seem, God is working in ways we often cannot see or understand.

Fifth, a Christian receives strength from God's presence. He has promised never to abandon His people, even in the worst of times. Romans 8:38 states,

> For I am convinced that neither death nor life, neither angels nor demons, neither the present nor the future, nor any powers, neither height nor depth, nor anything else in all creation, will be able to separate us from the love of God that is in Christ Jesus our Lord.

Sixth, there are valuable lessons to be learned from suffering. God will sometimes use evil to warn us and deter us from greater evils. In my teen-age years, I got into a minor fender bender shortly after receiving my driver's license. That experience created a healthy fear in me and has kept me from the greater evil of reckless driving.

There are some lessons we can only learn through our times of pain. As a high school and collegiate athlete, I endured the pain of training and repeated practice sessions. I knew that it was necessary to make me a better athlete. I would not be able to strengthen my body or increase my skill without the pain.

Trials do the same for us in regard to developing our character. The mettle of a person's character is tested, refined, and sharpened only when put through the fire of difficult trials. 1 Peter 1:6–9 states,

> In this you greatly rejoice, though now for a little while you may have had to suffer grief in all kinds of trials. These have come so that your faith—of greater worth than gold, which perishes even though refined by fire—may be proved genuine and may result in praise, glory and honor when Jesus Christ is revealed.

People of great moral integrity, who have touched our world in significant ways, endured some of the most difficult and painful experiences of life. The world is a better place because of Joni Erickson Tada, a quadriplegic, who inspired us to overcome our handicaps and live sacrificially for God and others. Corrie Ten Boom, Victor Frankel, and Deitrich Bonhoeffer's works have impacted the lives of millions because they persevered and overcame the horror of Nazi tyranny. Abraham Lincoln endured many hardships, the death of his mother at a young age, the death of three of his four children and other tragedies, but these made him a man of renowned moral character and courage. As a result of these people sharing their pain, we have a much greater depth of understanding of love, courage, faith, and character. This helps us become men and women of stronger character. For this reason James wrote,

> Consider it pure joy, my brothers, whenever you face trials of many kinds, because you know that the testing of your faith develops perseverance. Perseverance must finish its work so that you may be mature and complete, not lacking anything. (James 1:2-3)

In the context of a relationship with God, our suffering is not in vain, there is always a purpose. We cannot dispel the pain we experience, but we can overcome it through the power of Christ. We can draw comfort from knowing God cares for us as we receive strength from His presence. We have hope, knowing there is a purpose for our suffering, and that one day God will defeat evil and bring an everlasting rule of peace and justice. We will either go to be with the Lord at our death, or He will return and establish His rule forever. Either way, the Christian is victorious.

Chapter 9
See the Hope

*T*homas entered the doorway cautiously. He thought to himself, I *will not give way to their emotion. I love these men and we have been through a lot together, but I will not be convinced by their words. Unless I see, I will not believe.* With this determination, he entered and was embraced by the men.

"Thomas, we have seen Jesus!" they exclaimed. He was here among us! We touched Him and He showed us His hands and His side!" The excitement in that room was moving. A new sense of peace and joy had transformed these men. Thomas sensed something had happened, but life transformation was not the proof he was looking for.

Nathaniel, the once sarcastic one, was the first to invite Thomas to sit at the table and hear his story. The other men followed and as each one shared what they had witnessed, Thomas listened intently. He asked them detailed questions to find any inconsistency in their accounts. At the final question, the men waited for Thomas' response. He was fighting the emotions that wrestled in his heart. His friends were convincing in their accounts, but if he was going to surrender his life again to this Jesus, he needed to see a risen savior. *Unless I see, I cannot believe,* he thought to himself. As he gazed at his cup, the others waited to hear what their friend had to say.

Suddenly, they all gasped with elation as Jesus appeared in their midst. It was specifically for Thomas that He appeared this time. Thomas' eyes widened and his mouth dropped as he stared at Jesus. The fire of joy, excitement, and surprise raced through every cell of his body. This was not an illusion, this was real!

With love in his eyes, Jesus held out His hands to Thomas and gently said, "Put your finger here; see my hands. Reach out your hand and put it into my side. Stop doubting and believe."

Thomas slowly moved across the room and made his way to Jesus. He put his right hand on the nail mark in Jesus' left wrist first and then on His right. The wounds were healed but the inch-and-a-half-wide scars were still there. He then examined the pierced side of Jesus and saw the scar left by the Roman spear. It was about two and a half inches wide but fully healed.

With eyes the size of saucers, Thomas gazed into the eyes of God the Son and exclaimed, "My Lord and My God!" It was true, Jesus had risen and He was alive. As Thomas clung to Jesus' left hand, Jesus embraced him. Overwhelmed with joy, tears began to flow down Thomas' face. The other ten, cheering and rejoicing, gathered around the two. Then Jesus looked into the eyes of Thomas and said, "Because you have seen Me, you have believed; blessed are those who have not seen and yet have believed."

A small stack of books rested next to my floor cushion. I had read each book to examine the evidence for the Christian faith. I tested these facts by questioning professors and teachers who were skeptics. Many confident critics were unable to refute the evidence I presented and now the tables had turned. On a sunny May morning I finished the final chapter of *Know Why You Believe* by Paul Little and laid the book down. I buried my face in my hands and quietly whispered, "It's true. All of this is true." My search had come to an end. Jesus said, "You will know the truth and the truth shall set you free." I surrendered my life to Him and I was free. The evidence lay before me, this was not a mirage in the desert. The Bible was God's Word, Jesus was God incarnate and He had risen from the dead. I knew I would never look at life in the same way. Jesus stood before me with His arms stretched open and said, "Come. Put your finger here and feel the nail prints in my hands." I decided then that He would be my Lord and my God.

You Can Know God Personally

A dynamic relationship with God can be a reality in your life by believing the good news. This is the Gospel message: God loves you and desires to have a personal relationship with you. However, we cannot experience this love relationship because we have disobeyed God and chosen to live the way we desire with no regard for Him. This attitude is called sin and this separates us from God.

Although God is loving, He is just, and the price of sin is eternal separation from God, eternal death in hell. God in His love sent Jesus, God the Son, to die in our place and pay the penalty of sin. Justice has been fulfilled on the cross; the price of sin has been paid.

All that is required of us is:

1.   Confess or agree with God that we have sinned and express our sorrow for rejecting Him.
2.   Accept His offer of forgiveness by placing your trust in Jesus who died for your sins and rose again, conquering sin and death.
3.   Personally receive Jesus as your only Savior and Lord of your life.

If this is the desire of your heart, then pray this prayer. It is not just the words that bring you into relationship with God but the sincerity of your heart.

> Dear Jesus. I agree that I have sinned by choosing to live my way and rejecting You. I ask for forgiveness for my disobedience. Thank you for sending Jesus to pay the price of my sin. I believe He died in my place and rose again, conquering sin and death. Today I receive you as the Savior and Lord of my life. In Jesus' name, Amen.

If this is the sincere desire of your heart, you have become a new creation. Everything has now changed. Paul stated in 2 Corinthians 5:17, "Therefore, if anyone is in Christ, he is a new creation. The old has gone; the new has come."

You now have a personal relationship with God. John 1:12 states, "Yet to all who received Him, to those who believed in His name, He gave the right to become children of God." You have received the assurance of eternal life with God. John 5:24 states, "I tell you the truth, whoever hears My word and believes Him who sent Me has eternal life and will not be condemned; he has crossed over from death to life." The empowering presence of Christ will always remain with you; for He has indwelt you with His Holy Spirit to abide in your heart forever. Jesus stated in John 14:15–17, "If you love Me, you will obey what I command. And I will ask the Father, and He will give you another Counselor to be with you forever—the Spirit of Truth."

There are many more promises to be experienced in the new life of a believer. There is the promise of everlasting joy, everlasting peace, fullness of life, and much more. These can be found in God's Word, the Bible. It is my suggestion that you begin your new life in Christ with a daily Scripture reading beginning in the book of John. Knowing God does not mean one will have an easy and pain-free life. Trials and tribulations will come, but Jesus gives us the hope and the ability to overcome the difficulties we will face through the power of the risen Christ.

The hope of every man, woman, and child is found in a person, the person of Jesus Christ.

Conclusion

In my personal quest, Jesus revealed His nail pierced hands and wounded side to me. It is my sincere hope that He has done the same for you. This book is not an exhaustive work on the evidences for the Christian faith. This book was designed to confirm a Christian's beliefs and challenge unbelievers to consider the faith. For some, I am sure it answered their questions. For others I hope it piqued some interest to begin your own search for the truth.

Tradition teaches that Thomas became one of the greatest evangelists of the twelve disciples of Jesus. He ventured all the way to India to preach the message of the risen Jesus, of whom he had once refused to believe. There in India he died as a martyr. He was tied to a stake and run through with a lance. A church still exists there dedicated to this wonderful disciple whose honesty has led us to hear some of the greatest words ever taught by Jesus. Thomas' words, "Unless I see ..." have been shared by all those who search for the truth in the same manner.

For Further Study

I would like to recommend the following more extensive works written by some of the best Christian scholars:

More Evidence for the Christian Faith:
A Reasonable Faith by William Lane Craig
When Skeptics Ask by Norman Geisler
Mere Christianity by C. S. Lewis
The New Evidence That Demands a Verdict by Josh McDowell
Faith and Reason by Ronald Nash

Evidence for the Resurrection of Christ:
Who Moved the Stone? by Harold Morris
The Testimony of the Evangelists: The Gospels Examined by the Rules of Evidence, Simon Greenleaf, Royal Professor of Law, Harvard University.
The Case for Christ by Lee Strobel

Regarding Christianity and Science:
Intelligent Design by William Dembski
Darwin on Trial by Phillip Johnson
Evidence for Faith by John Warick Montgomery
The Creation Hypothesis by J. P. Moreland
The Creator and the Cosmos by Hugh Ross
Not a Chance by R. C. Sproul

Bibliography

Anderson, Norman. *Christianity and the World Religions.*
Downer's Grove, IL.: InterVarsity, 1996.

Bryce, Trevor. *The Kingdom of the Hittites.* Oxford: Clarendon Press, 1998.

Carson, Donald. *The Gagging of God: Christianity Confronts Pluralism.*
Grand Rapids, MI.: 1996.

Craig, William Lane. *Apologetics: An Introduction.*
Chicago: Moody Press, 1984.

Crossan, John. *Jesus: A Revolutionary Biography.*
San Francisco: Harper and Collins, 1989.

Douglas, J. D., ed. *New Bible Dictionary.* Wheaton, IL.:
Tyndale House Publishers, 1988.

Garstang, John. *The Foundations of Bible History*; Joshua, Judges.
London: Constable and Company, 1931.

_____. *The Land of the Hittites.* London: Constable and Company, 1910.

Geisler, Norman. *When Skeptics Ask.* Wheaton, IL.: Victor Press, 1989.

_____. *Baker Encyclopedia of Christian Apologetics.* Grand Rapids, MI.:
Baker Books, 1999.

Geisler, Norman, & Nix, William. *A General Introduction to the Bible.*
Chicago: Moody Press, 1986.

Glueck, Nelson. *Rivers in the Desert.* New York: Farrar, Strous and Cudahy,
1959.

Greenleaf, Simon. *The Testimony of the Evangelists; The Gospels Examined by
the Rules of Evidence.* Grand Rapids, MI: Kregal Publications, 1995.

Hoerth, Alfred. *Archaeology and the Old Testament.* Grand Rapids, MI:
Baker Book House, 1998.

Hume, David. *An Enquiry Concerning Human Understanding*. Oxford, England: Clarendon Press, 1902.

Jastrow, Robert. *God and the Astronomers*. New York: Norton & Company, 1978.

Kenyon, Kathleen and Holland, Thomas. *Excavations at Jericho Vol. 3: The Architecture and Stratigraphy of the Tell*, London: BSA p. 370.

_____. *Digging Up Jericho*. New York: Fredrick Praeger Publisher, 1957.

LaHaye, Tim. *Jesus, Who Is He?* Sisters, OR.: Multnomah Books, 1996.

Lecky, William. *History of European Morals from Augustus to Charlemagne*. New York: D. Appleton and Co., 1903. Page 8.

Lewis, C. S. *Mere Christianity*. New York: Macmillan Publishing, 1960.

_____. *Miracles*. New York: Macmillan Publishing, 1960.

_____. *The Problem of Pain*. New York: Macmillan Publishing, 1960.

Little, Paul. *Know Why You Believe*. Downers Grove, IL.: InterVarsity Press, 1988.

McDowell, Josh. *Evidence That Demands a Verdict*. San Bernadino, CA.: Here's Life Publishers, 1979.

_____. *More Evidence That Demands a Verdict*. San Bernadino, CA.: Here's Life Publishers, 1975.

_____. *The Resurrection Factor*. San Bernardino, CA.: Here's Life Publishers, 1981.

McRay, John. *Archaeology and the New Testament*. Grand Rapids, MI.: Baker Book House, 1991.

McNeill, William. *A World History*, Third Edition. New York: Oxford University Press, 1979.

Millard, Alan. *Nelson's Illustrated Wonders and Discoveries of the Bible*. Nashville: Thomas Nelson Publishers, 1997.

Montgomery, John, ed. *Evidence for Faith*. Dallas: Probe Books, 1991.

Morison, Frank. *Who Moved the Stone?* Grand Rapids, MI.: Zondervan Publishing, 1958.

Nash, Ronald. *Faith and Reason*. Grand Rapids, MI.: Zondervan Publishing, 1988.

_____. *Is Jesus the Only Savior?* Grand Rapids, MI.: Zondervan, 1994.

Netland, Harold. *Dissonant Voices*. Vancouver, British Colombia: Regent College Publishing, 1991.

Noss, John. *Man's Religions*. New York: Macmillan Company, 1956.

Okholm, Dennis. *Four Views on Salvation in a Pluralistic World*. Grand Rapids, MI.: Zondervan 1995.

Price, Randall. *The Stones Cry Out*. Eugene, OR.: Harvest House Publishers, 1997.

Probe Mind Games Notebook. Probe Ministries International, 1998.

Richard, Ramesh. *The Population of Heaven*. Chicago: Moody Press, 1994.

Richardson, Don. *Eternity in Their Hearts*. Ventura, CA.: Regal Books, 1981.

Ross, Hugh. *The Creator and the Cosmos*. Colorado Springs: NavPress Publishing, 1993.

Russell, Bertrand. *Religion and Science*. London: Oxford Press, 1961.

_____. *Why I Am Not a Christian*. New York: Simon & Schuster, 1957.

Stott, John. *Basic Christianity*. Downers Grove, IL.: Inter Varsity Press, 1971.

Strauss, David. *The Life of Jesus for the People*. Volume 1, Second Edition. London: Williams and Norgate, 1879.

Thangaraj, Thomas. *Relating to People of Other Religions*. Nashville: Abingdon Press, 1989.

Theide, Peter Carsten, and D'Ancona, Matthew. *Eyewitness to Jesus.* New York: Doubleday, 1996.

Unger, Merril. *Unger's Bible Dictionary.* Chicago: Moody Press, 1971.

Walvoord, John. *Prophecy Knowledge Handbook.* Wheaton, IL.: Victor Press, 1990.

Wright, Fred. *Highlights of Archaeology in the Bible Lands.* Chicago: Moody Press, 1955.

Yamauchi, Edwin. *The Stones and the Scriptures.* Philadelphia: J.B. Lippen Lott Company, 1972.

Periodicals

Arav, Rami , Richard Freund, and John Schroeder. "Bethsaida Rediscovered," *Biblical Archaeological Review*. January/February 2000, pp. 44-56.

Biblical Archaeological Review, March/April 1994, "David Found at Dan." pp. 26-39.

Corduan, Winfried. "General Revelation in World Religions." *Journal of Christian Apologetics*, Winter 1997, pp. 59-72.

Freedman, Noel and Geoghegan, Jeffrey. "House of David Is There!" *Biblical Archaeological Review*. March/April, 1995, pp. 78-79.

Lemonick, Michael. "Score One for the Bible." *Time*, 5 March 1990, p. 59.

_____. "Are the Bible Stories True?" *Time*, December 18, 1995, pp. 62-70.

Merril, Eugene. "The Very Stones Cry Out: A New Witness to an Ancient Record." *Gospel Herald at the Sunday School Times*, Fall 1995, pp. 54-55, 59.

Wilford, John. "Archaeologists say Evidence of House of David Found." *Dallas Morning News*, 6 August 1993, 1A and 11A.

Wood, Bryant. "Did the Israelites Conquer Jericho?" *Biblical Archaeological Review*, Vol. 16:2, 1990.

Work: Plato
When Written: 427–447 B.C.
Earliest Copy: 900 A.D.
Time Span: 1200 yrs.

Work: Thucydides
When Written: 460–400 B.C.
Earliest Copy: 900 A.D.
Time Span: 1300 yrs.

Work: Gallic Wars
When Written: 100–44 B.C.
Earliest Copy: 900 A.D.
Time Span: 1000 yrs.

Work: Tacitus
When Written: 100 A.D.
Earliest Copy: 1100 A.D.
Time Span: 1000 yrs.

Work: Aristotle
When Written: 384 B.C.
Earliest Copy: 1100 A.D.
Time Span: 1400 yrs.

Work: Iliad
When Written: 900 B.C.
Earliest Copy: 400 B.C.
Time Span: 500 yrs.

Work: New Testament
When Written: 50–100 A.D.
Earliest Copy: 125 A.D.
Time Span: 25 yrs.